Play

SECOND EDITION

Catherine Garvey

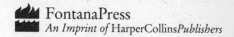
FontanaPress
An Imprint of HarperCollins*Publishers*

First issued in 1977 by Open Books,
in conjunction with Fontana,
an imprint of HarperCollins Publishers,
77–85 Fulham Palace Road,
Hammersmith, London W6 8JB
Five impressions printed

This enlarged Second Edition first published in
Great Britain by Fontana Press 1991

9 8 7 6 5 4 3 2 1

Printed and bound in Great Britain by
HarperCollins Manufacturing, Glasgow

Acknowledgments

Much of the research work for this book was supported by grants from the National Institute of Mental Health (United States Department of Health, Education and Welfare). The cooperation of the several nursery schools and their playful children, who must remain anonymous, is hereby gratefully acknowledged. I am also indebted to Rita Berndt, Sandra Bond, Robert Hogan, Alicia Lieberman, Clementine Kaufman, and Stuart Hulse for their helpful comments on earlier versions of the book. A special note of thanks is owed to Fred, an old but still imaginative cat who taught me a great deal about play.

C.G.

Contents

Preface to the Enlarged Edition

Play appeals to teachers, parents, social scientists, and children for the same reason—it affords unlimited possibilities for trying out new ideas and for elaborating, recombining, and reworking old ones in the light of new discoveries. Since the original publication of *Play*, several factors have combined to increase interest in this diverse realm of childhood activity. Changes in the economy, in life-styles, and in populations have resulted in a sizable increase in the demand for group child care, and the pressing need to provide for the welfare, education, and entertainment of growing numbers of young children from different types of backgrounds is one impetus for a renewed concern with the role of play in development. Another is the increased appreciation among social scientists of the possible interrelationship of play, especially pretend and social play, and children's well-being. Research on the growth of social competence, readiness for formal schooling, and the ability to cope with intrapersonal and interpersonal affect; on family relationships and processes; and on the problems of handicapped, disturbed, or developmentally delayed children have frequently involved studies of play activities or identified play as a positive influence in other areas of development.

Still another factor is the advances in apparently unrelated fields that have made it possible for researchers to undertake more detailed investigations of the communication, the metacommunication or signals about communication, and the social engagement of children at play and of the cognitive capabilities such behavior implies. Both the widespread use of videotaping for observational studies in homes, classrooms, and playgrounds and more sophisticated approaches to the analysis of conversation, social interaction, interpersonal relationships, and cultural differences are contributing to a growing understanding of play and its significance for the developing child. In addition, a relatively new appreciation of social play as a highly skilled interactional achievement in its own right is evident in the work of a number of investigators. This enlarged edition of *Play* presents some of these promising avenues of study and summarizes the findings of a number of recent investigations.

It contains two additional chapters and an updated selection of suggested reading. The new Chapter 9, "Learning to Play," comprises two sections. The first discusses the young child's earliest play experiences in the family and the role of parents and siblings in the child's discovery of the possibilities of play; recent observations have provided increasing evidence of social influences on the development of varieties of play. The second describes some of the characteristics of social pretending, a play activity that has come to be seen as far more complex and intriguing than was previously thought.

The new Chapter 10, "Play and the Real World," examines some of the numerous questions about the potentially important relationship between play and social or cognitive development. It discusses the ways in which gender identity and play styles may influence one another; the relationship between play and friendship and play and popularity, or peer status; and, finally, the similarities and possible connections between play and literate behavior, especially that exemplified in storytelling and narrative. Each of these topics is of practical concern to parents and educators. And each also touches on matters of real and immediate importance to children themselves, who are engaged in acquiring sex-appropriate play styles, who are trying to get along with peers and learning to have and to be a friend, and who are faced with new and increasingly specialized uses of language in school settings.

Play

1 / What Is Play?

The play of children may strike us at times as fragile and charming, rowdy and boisterous, ingenuous, just plain silly, or disturbingly perceptive in its portrayals of adult actions and attitudes. If we look more closely, however, we can discern patterns of amazing regularity and consistency. My aim in this book is to show child's play in a new way, to show its systematic and rule-governed nature, which is, at once, the product and the trace of man's biological heritage and his culture-creating capacity. Play is most frequent in a period of dramatically expanding knowledge of self, the physical and social world, and systems of communication; thus we might expect that play is intricately related to these areas of growth. I am particularly interested in relating the structures of play to the productive uses of language, since both are powerful influences on the child's construction of reality. But let us start at the beginning, with definitions.

An Oxford philosopher, caricatured (or immortalized) in Tom Stoppard's play *Jumpers*, found himself entangled in an exceedingly difficult question: "Does God exist?" he inquired. Realizing that the question was a stubborn one, he tried an often successful rhetorical ploy. He repeatedly rephrased the question, asking next, "What is God?" and finally, ungrammatically but incisively, "What are God?" Let us take up the problem of defining our subject matter with a similar tactic, and pose the question, "What are play?"

Consider this purely imaginary dialogue between a mother and her six-year-old son:

"Tom, I want to clean this room. Go out and play."

"What do you mean 'go out and play'?"

"You know what I mean."·

"No, I don't."

"Well, just go out and do whatever you do when you're having too much fun to come in to dinner."

"You mean toss the tennis ball against the garage? Finish painting my bike? Practice standing on my head? Tease Andy's sister? Check out the robin eggs?"

The conclusion of the dialogue, which might involve parental violence, is best omitted.

In everday conversation, it is generally unfair and provoking to ask for precise definitions of familiar words. But when a familiar concept like aggression, intelligence, or personality becomes an object of study, then it must be defined or delineated, at least clearly enough so that those who contribute to the study and those who may benefit from it know they are talking about the same thing. Play has been a particularly recalcitrant notion, but we must try to specify what the term means—at least as it is used in the following pages.

An infant shaking a rattle again and again, a kitten chasing its tail, a group of boys absorbed in a game of marbles, a girl preparing an elaborate feast for the inhabitants of a doll's house, a toddler gleefully running from its mother, girls skipping rope to a rhymed chant, a child finger painting, two monkeys taking turns at attacking and fleeing, a little boy spanking and scolding his stuffed bear—are all these events play? What characteristics do they have in common? Is there any feature unique to play? Is play in childhood related to adult play? to the play of young animals?

In everyday use of the term the central notion seems clear enough, but the fringes of the concept are fuzzy. Play, like Proteus, keeps changing shape. Different scholars have fastened on one or two of its characteristic forms and have offered a variety of theories to account for the origins, properties, and functions of these forms in the life of the individual or the group. For example, the fact that, almost universally, the young of higher species engage in playful behavior that resembles adult activities but is somehow incomplete or unperfected led one scholar to propose that play was instinctive, its function being to exercise skills necessary for adult life. Karl Groos, a philosopher, saw in the play-fighting of animals and the imitative behavior of children a preparation for adult performance. A psychologist, G. Stanley Hall, noting the same characteristics as well as the fact that playful behavior changes with age, proposed the "recapitulation" theory. This maintained that the play of children reflects the course of evolution from prehistoric hominids to the present. The history of the race is recapitulated in each child's development. Both theories were developed at the turn of the century and were heavily influenced by Darwin's concept of natural selection.

Sheer exuberance is another seemingly universal characteristic of much playful behavior. The young of higher species frolic, frisk, gallop, gambol, cavort, engage in mock combat, with every sign of pleasure and high spirits and with no apparent utilitarian objective. These boisterous forms of play suggested to Herbert Spencer an expenditure of surplus energy. In one of the earliest books on psychology, Spencer hypothesized that excess energy accumulates (as a normal product of the healthy nervous system) and must then be discharged. Where no pressing demand is made for survival (in hunting, fighting, or mating) the superabundance of energy is released in exercises that employ normal patterns of behavior but lack any immediate goal. Spencer attempted to specify a physiological process that could explain this aspect of play and to account not only for its presence in higher forms of life but for its manifestations in individual species as well.

These explanations—instinctive preparation, recapitulation, and surplus energy—have since been discarded or revised and adapted to more current theoretical positions, but the phenomena they attempted to explain (partial similarity to adult behavior, gradual acquisition of new forms of play, exuberant activity) are important aspects of play. And there are yet other aspects that have attracted investigators from different scientific and humanistic areas. For example, the fact that in pretending children often express indirectly or symbolically pressing worries or fears and repeat these themes again and again suggests a view of play as cathartic—an attempt to reexperience, and thereby to resolve or master, a difficult situation. This aspect of play has been of particular interest to psychiatrists and clinical psychologists.

The diversity of forms of play coupled with the different approaches to its study has led to a proliferation of ideas concerning the causes of play and the functions it may serve. However, basic to any theoretical position that attempts to answer questions concerning its causes or its role in the life of any creature, species, or society is the specification of the phenomenon in question. Succinctly put by Hughlings Jackson: "The study of the causes of things must be preceded by the study of the things caused." Accordingly, in this book I will describe the various aspects of young children's play before offering speculations about its causes or its functions in the course of development.

Certain descriptive characteristics of play are widely cited as critical to its definition. Most students of play would accept the following inventory:

(1) Play is pleasurable, enjoyable. Even when not actually accompanied by signs of mirth, it is still positively valued by the player.

(2) Play has no extrinsic goals. Its motivations are instrinsic and serve no other objectives. In fact, it is more an enjoyment of means than an effort devoted to some particular end. In utilitarian terms, it is inherently unproductive.

(3) Play is spontaneous and voluntary. It is not obligatory but is freely chosen by the player.

(4) Play involves some active engagement on the part of the player.

Each of these characteristics is partially typical of states other than play. Work or artistic endeavors are frequently pleasurable and often undertaken spontaneously, but both have a product of some sort: each is intended to change the real world in some perceptible way. The same is true of organized sports, especially professional or competitive sports. Lounging is often pleasurable, freely undertaken, and quite often has no specific goal (though one may rest in order to recuperate or just to avoid working). But it does not require active engagement. Just doing nothing, being bored, is usually not pleasurable. It neither engages the person nor has a predetermined product, though the state may be voluntary. Daydreaming is often conceived of as pleasurable and is usually voluntary, but the daydreamer is passive, not actively engaged.

The final item on the inventory of widely accepted characteristics is:

(5) Play has certain systematic relations to what is not play.

This last quality is the most intriguing one. If play were just a unique, isolated outcropping, a widespread but temporary and harmless aberration of childhood, then it would be interesting as a fact, perhaps, but the study of play would have little redeeming scientific value. However, play has been linked with creativity, problem solving, language learning, the development of social roles, and a number of other cognitive and social phenomena. The need to specify the nature of these links continues to motivate research.

The systematic relationships of play to what is not play carry an important implication that will be developed throughout this book. In fact, the very idea of play depends on contrast. We can only speak of play when we can contrast it with other orientations or states; we can only identify playful behavior when the actor can and does engage in corresponding but contrasting nonplayful behavior. The notion of contrast between play and nonplay and the fact that there are certain similarities between playful behavior and analogous nonplay behavior have influenced recent attempts to arrive at a working definition of play. It has become increasingly clear within the last decade that it is impossible to define play as a particular type or set of actions. Jumping, throwing a stone, chasing someone, even asking a question, or imitating another person's speech or movements can be performed as play but can also, of course, be performed in a nonplay fashion and with nonplayful intent. Some approach other than a simple inventory of play activities is obviously required.

One proposal has been made by Peter Reynolds, a specialist on the behavior of rhesus monkeys. He has suggested that play be considered "behavior in the simulative mode."[1] He observed that his monkey subjects displayed few action patterns (chase, present, mount, grab, or lunge) only in play and that few such patterns failed to occur in play. Taking into account the types of criteria used to identify and classify animal behavior (for example, physiological function, physical appearance, underlying mechanism in the nervous system, and effects on the environ ment), he suggested that behavior is organized into complex patterns he called "affective-behavioral systems." These are complexes of behavior, each one with its characteristic objectives and emotional orientations and typical outcomes. Feeding and mating are examples of such systems. Each system is linked to certain other systems—for instance, courtship normally precedes mating. When an affective-behavioral system (such as aggressive attack) is temporarily uncoupled from its usual relations to other systems, but still operates normally in respect to its own internal dynamics, it is functioning in the simulative mode. Play is an affective-behavioral system in its own right. It has, however, no particular behavior or objective unique to itself. Its behavior patterns are "borrowed" from other affective-behavioral systems. Thus, when the aggressive-attack system is transferred to the simulative mode for actual performance, the resulting behavior *resembles* a purposive attack. But the attacker performs his play-attack outside the context that might normally instigate attack, and he does not carry it through to its typical end. Reynolds suggests that simulation provides savings in both physiological and psychological energy to the young animal, and Jerome Bruner has also stressed the advantages of performances that are free, or "buffered," from normal consequences.[2]

In identifying an activity pattern as one performed in the simulative mode, we must necessarily rely on *contrasts* between the simulation and the behavior from which it derives. The contrasts may often be quite subtle—a fleeting grin or a quick wink may accompany an otherwise stinging verbal insult. Indeed, if we watch members of another species or culture, we may miss the contrast until we learn more about the system of communication within which it functions. Human beings tend to interpret behavior even as they see it. They assign meaning to behavior, classify it into conventionalized categories. It is these acts of categorization that permit behavior to be seen as meaningful, as I have proposed in another essay.[3] For example, if we see someone running and another person running a short way behind him, we would probably see these events as related and say that the first person was being chased by the second or that he was fleeing from the second. We might use other behavioral clues to infer guilt or anger on the part of the runners, to decide perhaps that one was a thief, and thus construct a "reasonable explanation" of their actions. This interpretation represents a *literal* orientation to the scene. (It might be changed to another literal interpretation if the next second we saw a rhinoceros charge around a corner after the runners.) But what if we heard one of the runners laugh or noted that they were smiling? Then we would likely decide that we were not witnessing a "real" pursuit, but that they were playing—or "just" playing, as we usually put it. We would have attributed a *nonliteral* orientation to the runners and constructed a nonliteral interpretation of what we saw. And just as we attribute meaning or intent to the actions of others, we conceive of our own behavior in similar terms: we interpret our actions and feelings as belonging to the same categories of intention, attitudes, and purposes, and entering into the same means-ends relationships, that we use to interpret the actions of others.

All play requires the players to understand that what is done is not what it appears to be. It is this nonliteral attitude that allows play to be buffered from its consequences: in effect, it permits play to be play. If play is a nonliteral orientation and playful behavior reflects that orientation, then we can ask: orientation to what, exactly?

RESOURCES FOR PLAY

Adult play is often quite complex, and several layers of significance may be present simultaneously. Further, much of what adults would call play has become "institutionalized"; there are fairly rigorous guidelines for selecting who may do it, when and where it is permissible, or how it is to be done. It is beyond the scope of this book to trace play forms through to adolescence or adulthood, but we may suppose that the aspects of play discussed below can exist even after childhood.

One widely accepted way of cutting up the universe of play makes the divisions at points where major changes in the child's growth become evident. Jean Piaget has divided play into three types.[4] Sensorimotor play, the first type, occupies the period from infancy through to the second year of life, when the child is busy acquiring control over his movements and learns to coordinate his gestures and his perception of their effects. Play at this stage often consists of repeating and varying motions. The infant derives pleasure from mastering motor skills and from experimenting with the world of touch and sight and sound. He takes joy in being able to cause events to recur. Symbolic or representational play is the second type, predominating after the age of two to about six. During this period a child acquires the ability to encode his experiences in symbols; images of events can be recalled. A child begins to play with symbols and their combinations, pretending, perhaps, to fill a nest with eggs as he piles marbles in a doll's hat. The third type of play is games with rules, which begins with the school years. The child has begun to understand certain social concepts of cooperation and competition; he is beginning to be able to work and to think more objectively. His play reflects this change as he is drawn to games that are structured by objective rules and may involve team or group activities.

This book, like some current work that will be discussed, departs from Piaget's formulation in two ways. In the first place I will examine specific types of play behavior and trace them through their lines of development. In the second, in contrast to approaches that stress the relation of play to the major changes in individual cognitive development, I emphasize the social nature of play from its beginnings: play with others is primary, and solitary play and private fantasy are secondary, derived ways of playing. The origins of most of the aspects of play can be detected, as I will attempt to show, in the earliest contacts of the child with his parents or caregivers. Although new ways of playing may be learned gradually and in other contexts, a nonliteral orientation to experiences is probably communicated to an infant within the first months of life.

Play takes many forms. One way of looking at its various aspects is to consider what material or resource is central: With what exactly is the child engaged? If it is true that a child can treat nonliterally whatever he has become familiar with—though not necessarily mastered—then new resources for play should appear as his world expands and becomes differentiated. It should be the case that as new abilities enter the repertoire through maturation or learning, or both, they become playable. As meaningful experiences are distinguished, they can be treated in a nonliteral fashion.

We will look at the aspects of play one by one, distinguishing them by the material or resource primarily involved. These resources are actually classes of experiences. They include motion and changes in perception resulting primarily from physical movement; objects and their physical as well as their combinational or associational properties; language and speech, which offer many levels of organization that can be turned to play; social materials, such as roles, situations, and attitudes—the various notions concerning the way the social world is constructed; and finally limits, where following rules or consciously breaking them is the primary resource for play. These aspects, the way they emerge and develop, their possible combination and integration into complex episodes of play, are my central topics.

RESEARCH PROCEDURES

Many examples of play in the following chapters are derived from an observational study of pairs of children in a single setting. The procedures were designed to provide examples of spontaneous behavior as little constrained as possible but in a setting that was the "same" for all the children. The principal objective of the study was a detailed analysis of children's activities in what was, potentially at least, a social situation. We asked these questions: To what extent do children interact with their peers in the absence of an adult? How does a child communicate with an agemate—that is, how is their conversation constructed? If the pair engages in social play, how exactly is it conducted?

These questions were formulated against a background of research that had emphasized the initial egocentrism of the preschool child in his thought and in his social life. During this period and up to the age of about eight, a child gradually "decenters." He becomes increasingly able to take the perspective of other persons, to understand not only that they may perceive, feel, and think differently from the way he does, but also to interpret their actions in different situations and to arrive at an understanding of what they may perceive, feel, or think. His actions and perceptions become less and less self-referenced. He learns to interact with people outside his family. He gradually moves from being a loner in play and work toward cooperation and teamwork.

Although this picture of the child is in some respects accurate, it is now apparent that emphasis on an understanding of decentering processes led researchers to neglect or ignore the social impulses and abilities that the child does actually possess—even at the very time that he can be accurately characterized as limited by his self-centeredness. But quite recently investigations have begun to search for the beginnings of children's discrimination of emotions in others, for the precursors of reciprocal, interpersonal communication, for the techniques whereby children engage and maintain interactions with their peers, and for the conditions under which children can accurately assess the perspective of another person. One example will indicate this shift in focus. From observations of children's behavior in a nursery school, Piaget noted that relatively little of the children's talk could be classified as "adapted" conversation—that is, as talk designed for and responsive to the informational needs of a particular listener. The children did not talk with one another so much as they engaged in noncommunicative repetitions, soliloquies, or collective monologuing, when everyone talked and no one listened. About 40 percent of four-year-olds' speech was found to be "egocentric," that proportion decreasing with age. In subsequent studies it has been shown that with age a child becomes increasingly better able to take his listener's needs into account.

A shift in research focus takes place when we ask: What about the other side of the coin? If 40 percent of the young child's speech is noncommunicative, what about the remaining 60 percent? Does adapted conversation resemble the speech of more mature speakers, or are children's conversations qualitatively different from those of skilled conversationalists? In respect to objective information exchange, we may ask: If the child does become more skilled in conveying information appropriate to the needs of his listener, how is it that even in his relatively unskilled period he manages to interact effectively, at least in some situations? What kind of "information" does he first learn to convey effectively, and under what conditions does improvement in communication skills first appear? In effect, the shift of emphasis reflects a renewed interest in the behavior of children as children, and it was in this climate of investigation that the work to be described here was undertaken.

We asked five private nursery schools serving a middle-class population in an eastern American city to select several sets of three children. Members of a set were of approximately the same age; were from the same class (and thus were acquainted with each other and the nursery school to much the same extent); and came from English-speaking homes. Each set was made up of either two girls and one boy or two boys and one girl. In all, forty-eight children took part in this study: four sets aged 2 years 10 months to 3 years 3 months (six girls and six boys); four, 3:6 to 4:4 (six girls and six boys); and eight, 4:7 to 5:7 (fifteen girls and nine boys).

Each set of three, accompanied by a nursery-school teacher, was welcomed by a young female researcher who escorted them to an office and relieved them of coats and boots. The researcher took the children to the water fountain and to the toilet and then invited them to draw straws to decide "who would get to go see the playroom first and who would get to play some games first." The child who drew the long straw went to another room with a young male researcher where he was given simple discrimination tasks and encouraged to talk about the miniature objects and pictures, or just to draw pictures if he preferred. The remaining two children were shown into the room where they would be observed. The pair of children was then left alone, and the teacher and researchers watched them from another room through one-way mirrors. A few sessions were briefly interrupted for a potty break or, if a child appeared concerned over the whereabouts of the teacher, to assure him that she was busy but would be along in a few minutes. Each pair remained in the room for about fifteen minutes. Then the third child was brought to the room, and one member of the pair turned to the discrimination tasks. In this way three pairs were formed in succession, and each child was observed with two different agemates.

The room in which the pairs were observed was furnished with a sofa, round movable table, carpet, curtains at the "windows," and bright pictures on the walls. In its center was a wooden box large enough for two children to sit on. It had a real automobile steering wheel and license plate, with four wheels painted on. Over this car was the microphone, which hung from a parrot on a perch. Placed about the room were a stool with a magnifying glass in the center; toy cars and trucks, ironing board and iron, stove with oven, dishes and pans, broom, tool-belt with pliers, hammer, and so on; a large stuffed snake, bear, fish, and tiger, a baby doll and cradle, blocks; a large cardboard box, suitcases, pocketbook, and lunchbox, all concealing jewelry, hats, shoes, shawls; and paper and colored pencils.

Each session was videotaped; all speech was transcribed in standard orthography, and a narrative account of the concurrent nonverbal behavior was prepared. Utterances (defined as stretches of one person's speech separated by the speech of the partner or separated by a pause exceeding one second) were numbered for ease of reference.

An interesting observation was made at the time of data collection. After the first two sets had visited the laboratory, we realized that, during the reception period, not one of the three children had spoken directly to another child, though most children talked quite freely with the adult researchers and the teacher. They did talk about one another, for instance "Johnny has a birthday today," but addressed their comments and questions about the new setting exclusively to the adults. Thereafter the researcher who welcomed the children carried a small tape recorder in her pocketbook during the reception period—to toilet, water fountain, and while getting coats off and on. We confirmed our initial impression, which was all the more striking in contrast with the extensive conversations that took place between the children themselves in the playroom. It appeared that the availability of adults had restricted the children's conversation with one another.

A second body of observations of agemates has been collected with similar procedures by Alicia Lieberman at the Johns Hopkins University. There were several ways in which the procedures and children used in her study differed from the study just described. Pairs (rather than triads) of same-sex, previously unacquainted children came to the laboratory at the same time. Half the subjects attended full-time day-care centers; half, part-time nursery schools. After their reception at the laboratory, however, the observation procedures, room, and furnishings were essentially the same. There were forty children in this study ranging in age from 3:0 to 3:6. The main objective of the research was to study individual differences in preschoolers' social competence when interacting with an unfamiliar child.

The majority of examples in this book are derived from my own work described above, but some are taken from the sessions collected by Lieberman. I will identify examples from both studies as "paired age-mate sessions" when it is necessary to distinguish them from illustrative material taken from other research. When comparisons between the behavior of the acquainted pairs and the unacquainted pairs are relevant, the two types of groups will be identified as such.

Analyses of the data derived from the acquainted pairs support the following conclusions:

(1) Pairs of children as young as three years were able to sustain a conversational interaction, though the length of such exchanges tended to increase with age. There were more episodes of focused interaction, that is—of mutual attending and responsiveness—than would be expected from the previous reports of solitary or parallel play in nursery schools. A number of conversation-building techniques were well controlled by even the youngest pairs. For example, one of these techniques is the ability to convey a request (A: *Give me that hammer*); express noncompliance (B: *I got it first*); paraphrase the unsuccessful request (A: *Well, I need it*); and negotiate the demand (B: *You can have the pliers.* A: *No, I'll give you the flashlight if you give me the hammer*).

A technique that was used for clarifying a misheard or a misunderstood utterance involved precise control of intonation. When one child didn't hear what the other had said, he would ask, ′*What* or ′*Huh*,* and thereby elicit a repetition from the other. If he failed to understand some part of the message he could ask‵*What* or‵*Who* and receive the specific information he needed. To compare these two common and essential procedures, consider these contrasting examples:

A: It doesn't work.   A: It doesn't work.
B: ′What?   B: ‵What?
A: It doesn't work.   A: The iron.

In the following chapters examples of play will illustrate many other ways in which the children exhibited conversational skills.

---

*Direction of pitch is indicated by a symbol placed immediately before the syllable that initiates a pitch change. ‵and‸ indicate high falling and low falling pitch; ′and, , high rising and low rising; and⌢and⌄indicate high rising-falling and low rising-falling pitch, respectively. Conventional punctuation is retained, though it is usually redundant given the pitch symbols.

(2) There was considerable variation in a child's social behavior depending in part on the behavior and compatibility of his partner. With a less talkative partner a child would speak less than he did with his other more loquacious partner. The success of play episodes also varied across pairs. Two children might jointly construct several complex make-believe episodes, but when one of the children was paired with his second partner, make-believe play might be fragmentary or virtually nonexistent. Further, the teachers reported that many of the children seemed far more peer-oriented and socially skilled in the age-mate sessions than at the nursery school or on the playground. Two factors may contribute to this effect: the absence of an adult and the reduction of the social and physical distractions generally found in nursery-school classes. It is likely that a pair comprises the most natural of social units. Basic patterns of exchange are first learned in the mother-infant pair. It may be that one must then *learn* to interact with more than one person at a time and must acquire techniques for dealing with persons whose speech and conversational habits are not well known. And in the laboratory playroom there was no distracting noise or interruption from other children's activities, which there clearly are even in the best-run nursery class or play group.

(3) Perhaps the most important result to emerge from this study is the overwhelming evidence that *not all that young children do together is play*. They have many modes of interacting, and they mark the play mode as distinct from other orientations. This may seem obvious on first reading since it is well known that children also fight and argue or often just watch each other. However, like many "obvious" facts this has been widely ignored, and we have as one consequence little information about how children actually do communicate with other children or transact their social affairs. The fact that the children in the paired agemate sessions moved back and forth among different activities and often changed their orientation to each other was most important, since it provided clear and often striking contrasts on which to base the descriptions of play as opposed to other orientations.

It has been proposed that the first functional distinction regarding the use of language is that between speaking and keeping silent. After that, of course, many other distinctions are made—

those that determine the choice of polite, humorous, or conde-
scending alternatives for speaking and acting, and so on. One of
the first functional discriminations in the perception of persons
is, most probably, that of familiar and unfamiliar. After that,
such distinctions as age, sex, and status are made and become
more and more influential in determining choices among the
available variants in the child's repertoire of behavior. From
examination of the videotapes made of the sessions we extracted
two very critical distinctions that appear to influence almost
everything a child does. We would expect these distinctions to be
made and used at a very early age, but certainly by the age of
three most children are able to verbalize their awareness of
whether they are playing or not and of whether they are alone or
are engaged with another person. Almost all of the videotaped
data could be classified into the four possible states that result
from the distinctions: play/nonplay and social/nonsocial. In
other words, a child could be playing or not playing and, in the
latter case, he could be doing nothing, or what we might call
problem solving, or engaging in talk that was neither playful nor
directed toward the solution of any immediate problem or difficulty. The existence of other orientations contributes to the
identification of play itself, which is thus marked as a special
state. This marking is particularly clear—and critical—when the
child is interacting with another child, for in that situation the
two must communicate to each other whether what is done is
done as play or as nonplay. Successful interaction between children depends on the participants' mutual awareness of whether
they are playing or not playing. The paired agemate sessions
provide a situation in which the intimate relationship between
play and communication is strikingly evident.

My examination of play in childhood begins with a brief discussion of the emergence of smiling and laughter, which are
common though not essential signals of a playful orientation.
The following chapters describe five aspects of play distinguished according to the resource with which the child is primarily engaged—for instance, motion, objects, or language. Next I
discuss a very special way of playing, with rules and rituals.
Finally, I conclude with a summary of the major points and with
some proposals concerning the functions of play in childhood.

2 / The Natural History of the Smile

The development of smiling parallels that of play. Compared to play, however, smiling has a fairly constant form. It can be observed, described, and reliably identified; it can be elicited and its immediate antecedents can be manipulated in order to determine what encourages or discourages its appearance. What is known about smiling mirrors some of the important characteristics of play.

An infant's first smiles are faint and fleeting and appear in the absence of any external stimulation. Endogenous, or internally triggered, smiles occur primarily during sleep and are believed to reflect mild changes in physiological excitation. A clearer, more positive smile in response to external stimulation (the exogenous smile) begins to appear in waking states at about three weeks of age. This smile, which is marked by crinkling around the eyes as well as a broader upturning of the lips, reflects the infant's attention to changes in his environment. However, the stimulation must be relatively mild or he will startle. What elicits a smile—that is, the type, intensity, and complexity of the stimulation—changes with maturation. During the third week of life it is the female voice that is most consistently effective. After the first month an infant will indicate his pleased attention at a silent moving face. Soon after the second month most infants will smile broadly at a round of Pat-a-Cake.

Not long after the exogenous smile appears, there is evidence that an infant begins to participate actively in creating and sustaining the states of stimulation that lead to smiling. What strikes him as amusing now appears to involve not only sound or motion as such but some contrast between expectation and perception. A familiar phenomenon, distorted or exaggerated in some way, now elicits smiles or laughter. Mother walking like a penguin or wearing a mask is funny, and repetition of such events usually produces a smile or a laugh. The timing of these responses indicates anticipation of the previously experienced outcome. An older infant is willing and able to participate in producing humor. The conditions under which he does so indicate the rapidly increasing role of his own interpretation and evaluation of potentially amusing events. According to Alan Sroufe, a psychologist who has traced this development of smiling and laughter through the first year of life, an infant tends to be attracted to the incongruous—what he does not quite understand. If he can interpret a novel event as nonthreatening, then he will laugh or smile. As he matures, he becomes increasingly active in producing and mastering new experiences that generate amusement.[1]

The smile grows from a faint grimace to a broad grin. Chortles, laughs, chuckles, and guffaws come later but do not, of course, replace smiling. What elicits such responses becomes increasingly differentiated until by early childhood a number of different classes of events are effective. In what may be one of the most delightful experiments in the history of psychology (a discipline not usually given to amusing treatment of its subject matter), Florence Justin attempted in 1932 to discover the immediate causes for laughter in children.[2] She set out to test various theories of the antecedents of laughter, among which were theories that laughter resulted from surprise or a defeated expectation; a feeling of superiority at another's misfortune or ineptness; release from strain or tension; perception of incongruity and contrast; seeing another person laugh or indicate that something was funny; and engaging in verbal or physical play.

Justin's techniques for eliciting laughter from children aged three, four, five, and six were ingenious. For example, interviewing one child at a time amid a number of props, she announced that she would boil an egg in a pan of water and time it with a watch. Then she dropped the watch in the hot water and consulted the egg. Next she invited the child to join her for a story session, pulled up a small chair, started to sit down, missed the chair, and tumbled onto the floor. These happenings were used to test the superiority-degradation theory. To test the surprise theory, she presented three little covered buckets. The child inserted his hand through a slit to find sand in one, water in the next, and in the third, nothing. To test the strain theory, a child walked a narrow line carrying a parasol and a potato in a spoon. The social smile was elicited by the experimenter smiling and laughing herself, tacitly inviting a response by the child.

Justin found that all the conditions elicited smiling or laughter from each age group. From 40 to 95 percent of the children in each group smiled in each of the situations, but older children responded to a greater variety of incidents and tended to smile longer. According to the length of the responses and to the percentage of children giving a response to each condition, relief from strain or tension and superiority-degradation were least effective. The social-smile situation was highly effective, even for the three-year-olds. There was a slight tendency for children to laugh more at situations in which they participated directly. Justin's study suggests that by the age of three most adult forms of mirth are foreshadowed but that "the field of the laughable is being constantly extended." She attributed the enlargement of the field of laughter-provoking incidents to the processes of mental growth.

Investigation of the immediate contexts of smiles and laughter in the paired agemate sessions of acquainted children suggests that at least as many types of conditions are effective in producing spontaneous humor responses as those used by Florence Justin. Further, laughter or giggles also appeared to serve such social functions as attracting a partner's attention, enticing him to join in some activity, or marking what one had just done as "funny." There were several instances in which an apparently aggressive gesture (like snatching an object from a partner or threatening with raised arm and clenched fist) was accompanied by exaggerated laughter. In these cases the marker of playful intent was generally effective in that the partner did not respond defensively. For the preschool age child, then, smiles and laughter have become an important part of the complex system of signals he can send and interpret when interacting with others.

Smiling is universal in our species, which has been called *homo ludens.** It would follow that smiling has some physiological basis and that it plays or has played some role in the evolu-

*There is some question as to whether anthropoids smile, although a smilelike expression has been observed under certain conditions in apes, most notably when they were watching young human children.

tion of the species. The psychophysiological basis for the smile is thought to be a process of tension-relaxation. This happens when the infant encounters something novel or unusual. First he freezes and gives it all his attention. Then, if he finds it threatening or unpleasant, he will cry or perhaps move away; if not, the tension evaporates and he will smile, laugh, or perhaps even approach or reach out. The important point here is that it is his *evaluation* of the event, person, or object as interesting but not threatening that tips the balance toward smiling or laughter.

Studies of smiling and laughter have shown that infants and young children are sensitive to various dimensions of social settings. Researchers have found that, while laughter would be elicited at five weeks in the home, it could not be called forth in the laboratory until twelve or sixteen weeks. Children of one year would respond to tickling by parents in a laboratory, but would not laugh if tickled by the experimenter. At about the same time the approach of a strange child might elicit a smile, whereas the approach of a strange adult would probably produce some negative reaction.

A young infant's smile on the appearance of its mother has been called a smile of recognition. It begins to appear at about three months and is generally overinterpreted by the mother to mean "he recognizes *me*." Naturally, this "greeting" evokes a strong maternal response in her. If the expression was instinctive at first, it now enters into a system of social interactions in which the behavior of each participant is influenced by that of the other. It appears that prolonging an infant's smiling or laughter is extremely satisfying for parents. Smiling and laughter, then, have not only evaluative and expressive functions, but are important in initiating and maintaining early communicative exchanges. Adults often work indefatigably to bring forth smiles and laughter in their young, and a healthy baby soon learns how to keep his parents performing in an amusing way. It is increasingly clear that in the infant's early pleasurable encounters he is more than a pleased, passive audience. He actively invites certain diversions and rejects others.

By nursery-school age, a child is able to find many different classes of phenomena amusing or delightful. He has a range of responses—smiling, laughing, giggling—and this range probably reflects the qualitative or quantitative distinctions he can make among amusing events. Further, he can discriminate certain aspects of social situations (setting, and the age, number, and familiarity of the people involved) which influence his evaluation of what is funny and the kind of response he is likely to produce. It is this last fact that has posed problems for investigations of children's understanding and enjoyment of humor. Signs of amusement may be inhibited in an experimental situation and even the stimulus—a joke or cartoon—may elicit a problem-solving approach instead of mirth. Conversely, what is evaluated as funny and the intensity of the overt response can be positively influenced by the social situation. And the threshhold for delight and its expression can be dramatically lowered for children by the sheer presence of other children.

GROUP GLEE

A fascinating phenomenon, long familiar to nursery-school teachers, has recently been discussed and named for the scientific community by Lawrence Sherman.[3] That phenomenon is "group glee," the spontaneous eruption of mirth among children. It manifests itself in a sudden wave of screams or giggles, and often involves jumping up and down and hand-clapping. It appears to possess all the children simultaneously or spreads like wildfire from one child through the group. Over a two-year period, Sherman observed 596 directed-activity sessions lasting about twenty minutes. Group size in the nursery school was small (three to four), medium (five to six), and large (seven to nine). The sessions were made up of children of the ages of three, four, and five. In all, 633 outbreaks of group glee were observed.

The immediate antecedents of group glee, Sherman found, were quite varied. Four were similar to the antecedents of laughter: intense physical activity such as dancing; an incongruent perception—as when one child called a teddy bear a "teddy dog"; taboo breaking with "bad words," or rule transgression; and perception of another's misfortune—as when one child tripped over a milk carton. However, other events or situations could also trigger group glee. The most effective of these were volunteering—for example, the teacher asked "Who wants to go outside and get John?" and the children shouted "Me, me me . . ."; termination of a situation, such as the end of a story session; announcement of a future event; and unstructured situations—as when children were left waiting before a planned activity began. An episode of group glee is likely to last less than nine seconds and tends to occur more frequently in the larger groups and in mixed rather than in same-sex groups. All age groups engaged in this behavior to about the same extent. (Teachers acted to suppress gleeful explosions when these occurred during a lesson activity and particularly when they *spread* throughout the group [rather than erupting simultaneously in the entire group]. Otherwise they generally tolerated them.)

Do experiences of group glee in a nursery class contribute to learning and retention of lesson materials, or to the willingness of the classmates to cooperate with the teacher and with each other? One might speculate that the answer would be yes.

Although smiles and laughter are overt behavior, whereas play is an attitude or orientation that can manifest itself in numerous different kinds of behavior, this brief account of smiling, laughter, and glee reveals many similarities to the development of play. First, from early vague gestures, the signs of mirth become increasingly differentiated and clear. Similarly, it is difficult to be quite sure that many infant activities reflect a playful orientation. Probably a very young child is himself not consistently aware of the distinction between play and nonplay in many of his own activities. Certainly he often fails to perceive that distinction in other people's activities. Second, just as a child becomes more active in creating the conditions for a humor response, so does he become more active in play—moving, for example, from an audience role in Peek-a-Boo to an active role by covering his own or his mother's face. In smiling and in playing, the growth of voluntary control is reflected in important changes in the organization of behavior. Third, as a child grows, so does the field of the risible; the nature of what can be appreciated becomes more complex, more varied, and more intellectual. What can be played expands as new areas of experience are encountered and appropriated for playful purposes. Fourth, laughter as a sign of joy and play behavior are both likely to appear under conditions of well-being. The sick, bewildered, frightened child does not smile or play.

Fifth, and finally, smiling and playing come under the influence of social and environmental factors virtually from their beginnings. Both are highly social in their earliest periods and are shaped thereafter by interpersonal and environmental contingencies. Both smiling and playing are implicated in the child's first experiences of mutually shared attention and awareness with his parents and become more and more systematically linked with communicative exchanges. Through childhood and beyond, smiling and playing continue to have important ties with social phenomena; their occurrence is in part dependent on social factors such as familiarity and group size. Further, many aspects of children's play are also sensitive to the sex composition of the group.

Thus there are several interesting parallels between play and the development of smiling and laughter. But a word of caution is necessary. Not all manifestations of play are marked by grins or giggles, and a smile is by no means a reliable index of a playful orientation. It is characteristic of human behavior that there are few, if any, simple and constant relations between a gesture and its meaning or significance in a communicative situation.

3 / Play with Motion and Interaction

The kind of play that most clearly reflects exuberance and high spirits is based on the resource of motion. The running, jumping, skipping, shrieking, and laughing of children at recess or after school is joyous, free, and almost contagious in its expression of well-being. Although it is an aspect of play that has received considerable study, a number of unanswered questions remain. One concerns the development of play with motion in its solitary appearances and in its more boisterous manifestations in groups.

Motion, the sensations of movement and the changing sensations that motion produces, are the first amusements adults offer to infants. Babies are jiggled up and down on the knee, tickled or repeatedly hoisted high in the air, and they show evident signs of pleasure in such experiences. And motion and changing sensations are also the first resources for play that an infant himself can exploit alone during the time he is discovering his ability to control his movements. Piaget provides an example of a solitary infant's discovery of a voluntary movement—tilting his head back. At first the baby used this movement to provide a new view of familiar things but thereafter used his achievement playfully. In Piaget's words, the infant "seemed to repeat this movement with ever-increasing enjoyment and ever-decreasing interest in the external result: he brought his head back to the upright position and then threw it back again time after time, laughing loudly."[1] Such early episodes have in common with later and diverse types of play the fact that they are enjoyed for their own sake and are divorced from other goals they might normally serve.

25

There are problems in identifying segments of infant behavior as playful. Few of a young infant's movements are sufficiently well controlled to provide clear contrasts between accidental and voluntary behavior. One generally infers that an exchange between an infant and an adult is playful on the basis of their combined behavior. The repetition of movements and displacement of a particular movement from its normal role in a seemingly purposeful sequence of activity are the criteria most often cited as criteria for infant play. By late infancy or early childhood, sequences of skilled movements have developed and can be repeated or shifted from their usual place in a sequence. Furthermore, children have learned how to signal their playful attitude more clearly. Taken together, these developments permit more reliable identification of play.

Not even in the first four months, however, does an infant receive playful adult attention *passively*. Entertainment through motion and sensation may be offered by parents, but the infant takes part. The early play of an infant and its parent has an intrinsic goal that Daniel Stern has described as "pure interaction."[2] The means by which parents can create and maintain an optimal level of attention and arousal in an infant (whose obvious signals of pleasure further promote their efforts) consist of sounds, facial expressions, and movements, often including physical contact. A parent can vary these in speed, intensity, scope, and combination, producing changing and varied sensations. Close observations of infant and parent together suggest that elements of the parent's repertoire become grouped into distinctive, repeatable sequences—some of which can be named, like Pat-a-Cake. Within these sequences, the speed, range, and intensity of the parent's actions are to a large extent controlled by the infant's behavior. The infant's behavior is that action he can best control, his direction of gaze.* He averts his gaze or directs it to his parent, thus regulating the amount of stimulation he receives as well as influencing the entertainer's performance.

An older infant soon produces motion and changing sensa-

---

*A very young infant is strongly predisposed to look at his partner's eyes, but this tendency soon becomes part of a system of interaction as well as a means of adjusting his internal state of arousal. Gaze will later serve as an important part of the more mature nonverbal communication systems he will acquire.

tions more directly in explorations of his environment. As an action pattern is "discovered," it is liable to be repeated and exercised, both for the pleasure of the experience and also to test and extend its immediate consequences. These playful explorations with motion, insofar as they have been described, do not appear to be shared with agemates until well into the second year of life. With cooperative and sensitive adults, however, an older infant takes an increasingly active role in playful activities, often initiating a sequence by himself producing the first move of a familiar game. But although play with motion has social roots in the infant-parent pair, it is not shared with agemates for some period of time to come. The earliest systematic studies of social play with motion begin in nursery school at about the age of three, though there is some evidence that still younger children can interact using alternating, repetitive patterns of physical actions, such as following and leading or imitating one another's movements.

ANIMALS' PLAY

Play involving motion and sensation is of considerable interest in its own right not only because of its prevalence in the healthy child (and thus its probable role in normal development) but also because it is the only aspect of play, to our best knowledge, that is displayed by both animals and human beings. Play in animals has long fascinated naturalists, zoologists, and ethologists. The question of its role in the development of individual animals and of species, in socialization processes and in the ecology of the group, is being researched with renewed interest. It is not surprising that recent study of children's spontaneous physical activities has been conducted primarily with procedures and theoretical orientations from the field of animal ethology. Ethologists believe that play increases the chances of survival for the individual as well as for the group, and that its long-range benefits are best discovered by detailed study of creatures in their natural environment. However, ethologists also arrange, judiciously and with minimal disruption, environmental factors in order to test hypotheses developed from their naturalistic observations.

Irenäus Eibl-Eibesfeldt wrote that "Play is an experimental

dialogue with the environment."[3] Some animals (generally those of "lower species") do not so much conduct a dialogue as follow a set script. Those species that are highly specialized to their specific environments, such as ants or bees, show little, if any, play. Instead play seems to be associated with the potentiality for adapting to changing circumstances. The more flexible an animal is, the more likely it is to play. In fact, Peter Reynolds suggests that a group of phenomena he calls the "flexibility complex" underlies the tendency of the young of a species to play or not. The flexibility complex includes a relatively long period of maturation and dependency on a caregiver, an increased ability to manipulate objects and use them as instruments; an increased reliance on learning by observation—acquiring information from watching others and observing what precedes and follows from their actions; the development of conventional action sequences built on *imitated* behavior; and the development of peer groups in the young and subsequent elaboration of social structures within adolescent subcultures.

The phrase "experimental dialogue" suggests a conversation in which one can take back what is said. Play behavior is, to a considerable extent, revocable. What is done in play is "uncoupled" from the typical consequences of analogous nonplay behavior; thus play provides an opportunity for the relatively safe, or minimally risky, exercise of new behavior in familiar situations, or of familiar behavior in new physical or social contexts. Also, play in animals tends to decline in adolescence and few adults engage in play (except sometimes with their immature young). It is thus likely that the functions of play are closely related to learning and early development. Since the environment is social as well as physical, in addition to integrating their behavior and testing its effect on their physical world, playing animals are learning to "talk" with other members of their groups and to understand one another's signals.

The word "experimental" further suggests curiosity, interest in what is novel or poorly understood. This attitude, sometimes called exploratory, is characteristic of the healthy young of most higher animals. Although we shall see in the next chapter that exploration and play differ in form and conduct, it is nevertheless true that the two are often temporally sequenced. A new experience, if not frightening, is likely first to attract attention, then exploration. Only after a novel feature of the environment has been investigated can it be treated more lightly and enjoyed. In respect to play with motion, there is a close link between exploration and the beginnings of interaction with contemporaries. Agemates are one of the most interesting features of the environment. They differ both from the caregiver and from inanimate things. They attract attention and often investigation because they move and do interesting and unexpected things. Harry Harlow and his colleagues, who have devoted many years to the study of young rhesus monkeys, have observed that play with peers begins as an extension of exploration and play with inanimate objects.[4]

The peak period of play in young animals is more often social than solitary. Since much (though not all) of the behavior exhibited by playing animals also appears later in mature mating, hunting, or fighting, ethologists have emphasized the relations of play to other kinds of action and interaction.* They not only view play as a type of communication but are also interested in the distinctive signals that differentiate playful behavior from the analogous nonplay activities. Thus two basic questions are asked: How do the changing forms of play relate to the life of the animal? How is behavior marked as playful, that is, how is a play orientation communicated within the group?

Two studies of play in animals will illustrate the ethological approach and suggest some ideas concerning the possible functions of play that emerge from this perspective. Meredith West observed twenty-eight domestic cats from fourteen days of age to maturity.[5] Six litters of kittens were kept with their mothers, three litters in a laboratory, and three in a home where they had unlimited access to the outdoors. She also observed three wild mothers and their seven young. During the hour and a half of daily observation, the behavior of each kitten was sampled. Preliminary work resulted in the identification of eight categories of movement patterns. The patterns, themselves complex clusters of behavior, formed the building blocks of longer sequences of

*It is interesting that play is assumed to be possible only among members of the same species, except for man with his pets or animals he has cared for. Few observations have been made of cross-species play, which does occur though only perhaps among domesticated animals who are house, yard, or pasture mates.

interaction. The aptness of the patterns she identified as units is confirmed by their role in the kitten's developing social activity. Briefly, the patterns and the age at which each was first observed were as follows:

Age first seen (in days)	Pattern
33-35	*Pounce.* Crouch with head low; back legs tucked in; hindquarters sway; thrust of forward movement is from extension of hind legs; tail straight back and may move back and forth.
32-34	*Side-step.* Arched back; tail curled up; walks sideways toward or around object or other kitten.
21-23	*Belly-up.* Kitten on back; all paws semi-vertical; hind legs treading, front legs pawing; teeth exposed; tail straight back or may move back and forth.
23-26	*Stand-up.* Stands near or over other kitten, head toward head or neck of other.
42-48	*Face-off.* Sits, hunched forward, eyes oriented to other kitten; lifts front paw forward, tail moves back and forth.
35-38	*Vertical stance.* Sitting position; rocks back on haunches and lifts front paws and stretches them perpendicular to its own body.
41-46	*Horizontal leap.* Lateral position relative to other kitten; back arched, curves tail upward and leaps off ground.
38-41	*Chase.* One kitten runs after (pursuit) or from (flight) another kitten.

These patterns appeared first in a solitary context and some appeared later than others. All were exercised repeatedly as they were first acquired. Then all the patterns began to be joined into sequences, with the number of joined patterns increasing from 4.8 per sequence at six weeks to 8.1 per sequence at twelve weeks.

The most favored opening move in a sequence was the pounce; the second, the side-step. Pounce never ended a bout and was never used as a response to an initial move. Belly-up and stand-up occurred most often in the middle of a sequence, with kittens rapidly exchanging these two complementary positions. Play episodes were usually terminated with a chase. The horizontal leap was the second most frequent termination, but it never started a play bout.

From five weeks play was primarily social. The number of bouts per hour started to increase at five to seven weeks and then from eight to sixteen weeks leveled off at about twelve. Subsequently the amount of social play declined sharply, as did other social activities such as mutual grooming.

A number of changes began to take place around four months of age. The homelife of the kittens began to break up, and they became much more individualistic. They slept more and spent much of their waking time in quiet, alert watching. The house-reared kittens spent most of their time outdoors, exploring and hunting. The males began to display sexual interest at about four and a half months but were rejected and avoided by the females, who did not respond to their advances until five and a half months. Each of the three wild mothers abandoned their kittens at around four months of age, and the littermates who had stayed together in their shelters then began to disperse and to hunt. The changes in play and other behavior were similar for the laboratory cats, who were not forced to obtain their own food and could not roam outdoors. Solitary play also declined, though more slowly, and some of the adults did occasionally play alone with objects.

West points out that several different types of signals can communicate a playful orientation. For example, tail movements in play are broader or more rapid than the analogous movements in neutral or aggressive contexts. Also, though some of the same configurations of movements are used both in play and in fighting, they are structured differently in the two states.

Play is vigorous exercise, it entails close contact with partners and especially one partner at a time, and it declines at the time when litters disperse and the young cats begin to turn their attention to other activities directed to survival (hunting, watching, or mating)—all this indicates that play is an integral and adaptive part of feline development. Since not all feline movement patterns are used in play and since there are also other kinds of social interactions such as grooming, play is by no means the single source of cat expertise, but it does appear to contribute to kittens' social harmony at a time when the litter is dependent on the mother and must stay together.

These observations suggest that play has many functions, and that its forms and periods of predominance are closely tied to the kittens' adaptation to their unique way of life. Some, though not all, of the movement patterns practiced in play are similar to patterns later specialized for hunting and fighting. Other species of animals play in very different ways which are compatible with their particular life style and with their mature nonplay activities. Marc Bekoff's studies of coyotes, beagles, wolves, and hybrids of these animals indicate that, even among these related species, there are striking differences in early social relationships.[6]

Bekoff, like West, developed a list of behavioral components and observed their occurrence and sequence in interactive episodes within pairs of pups. Contrasts between play and nonplay behavior were marked by exaggeration, by different sequences, and by certain movements and vocalizations that occurred uniquely in play. In all the pairs observed, as in the litters of kittens, close contact play preceded running and chasing. But preferred play-initiating moves differed not only from those of the kittens; they also differed among the three species studied.

Beagles were the most playful, wolves somewhat less so, and coyotes played relatively little. As early as twenty-one days of age, coyotes fought seriously. Their social relationships were first established by threatening and fighting, and only thereafter did some play appear. Wolves established their dominance patterns less violently by means of threats and began to play more at about one and a half months of age. Beagles did not engage in fighting, and their organization was quite democratic. Bekoff believes that these patterns of infant interactions are closely related to the beagle's domestication for hunting in groups or packs, to the wolf's cooperative group hunting and living arrangements, and to the coyote's more solitary adult life style.

A favorite beagle play initiation (two or more high leaps directed toward the prospective partner) was also displayed by hybrids derived from mating a coyote or wolf with a domestic dog. All hybrids used leaping as an invitation to play. This pattern has never been observed in coyotes and only rarely in wolves. Hybrids with a wolf parent used leaping more and at an earlier age than did hybrids with a coyote parent. Bekoff also found that the patterns (other than those ending in bouts) were clearly marked as playful. If two apparently conflicting markers occurred together, for example teeth bared (usually a signal of threat) with face-oriented pawing (usually an invitation to play), priority was given to the play signal.

From these two studies, it is clear that communication is an important factor in the social play of animals. Further, the studies support the ideas that play with motion can be reliably identified by contrast with other activity and that, even though species (and breeds) may differ in their forms of signaling, a playful orientation is marked as such. Further, play with motion for most animal species sometimes peaks before maturity, is most often conducted socially, and supports the maintenance of relations among littermates. The existence of specific action patterns, unique to a species, and the different frequency of play between species or breeds suggest a close tie with adult survival behavior and with the life styles of both young and adult animals.

The above also holds true for young primates reared in colonies or in nuclear families with access to others of the same age. As compared with the domestic cats or dogs, primates mature more slowly and remain longer with their mothers; they characteristically begin to play with agemates rather later. For many primates, there is a transitional period from mother-infant relations to playful peer relations. Rhesus monkeys first play alone and begin to contact others at about two months of age, but they take some time to learn how to play together. According to Harlow, their solitary play patterns are the precursors of the numerous interactive play responses that begin to appear after several months. The young rhesus eventually build up complex patterns for social encounters and also display special signals, such as open-mouthed facial expressions and a bounding gait, to indicate their playful orientation. By eight months, play has become the major social activity. Play encounters last longer as age increases, but in maturity play is largely replaced by more businesslike concerns. Rhesus monkeys deprived throughout infancy of contact with agemates have difficulty joining a group as adolescents; they are socially awkward or overly aggressive. They have failed to learn the patterns and signals of the group and are unable to make or to interpret the intention movements characteristic of its members. An important step in normal rhesus socialization is learning to play with peers.

THE BEGINNINGS OF SOCIAL PLAY IN CHILDREN

The young human, too, must learn to play with others like himself. His earlier play with parents depended on their willingness to structure predictable sequences of sound, touch, and motion, and to carry much more than half the burden of communication. Other children differ from both adults and objects in being less controllable and less predictable. Although one young child may find another very interesting, he does not quite know what can be done with him. Observations of children in play groups during the second year of life show that, when familiar adults are present, children are attracted to their peers. They spend a great deal of time watching each other's activities. There are, however, somewhat conflicting findings concerning the amount and type of social contacts that take place between ten months and two years.

Several studies have put children together in a situation in which their mothers were present but were instructed to talk naturally with each other and not to initiate any interaction with the toddlers. Carol Eckerman combined foursomes of same-age toddlers and their mothers and assessed how much activity they directed toward one another in a twenty-minute period (pairs were aged ten months to a year, eighteen to twenty months, or twenty-two months to two years).[7] Interaction between the children (as opposed to solitary activities or contacts with mother) increased after twenty months, and it took the form of mutual involvement with objects and direct involvement in one another's play: positive interaction (imitating or exchanging toys) was more frequent than negative (struggling). Edward Mueller observed a small play group of boys over several months and found that the focus of activity gradually shifted from objects to other children.[8] By eighteen months several children had learned how to cooperate and take turns with a playmate in both complementary sequences (alternating leading and following) and in imitative ones (reproducing the way another child handled an object).

Wanda Bronson, however, reporting on a study still in prog

ress, has observed very little change in how much infants initiate encounters with one another between ten months and two years, even though, like Mueller, she observed the same children over time.[9] Bronson's play groups were composed of three or four agemates (as was Mueller's single group) and, in all, forty children participated. She attributes the consistently low level of interaction between children of this age to their more compelling interest in the toys and objects in the room. Toddlers may be attracted to other toddlers, she suggests, but on investigation they find them too erratic to take many chances with. They snatch toys and are likely to cry or scream or poke at one. (About 45 percent of these children's brief encounters at each age ranged from mild to distressful disagreements or struggles.) The parent, it seems, remains the best person with whom to share toys and new sights and experiences. But Bronson did find qualitative changes in their behavior together. As the children became socially versatile, encounters became less transient, less tentative and "accidental." Disagreements did become more intense, though there were also more incidents involving cooperation or affection. These included offering objects, handling a toy together, and taking turns in brief bouts of Hide-and-Seek.

We can conclude that a two-year-old still has a great deal to learn about how to play with others. His social expertise rests on his experience with cooperative adults, and he must now learn how to sustain a mutually enjoyable encounter with a volatile and equally inept playmate. Human infants and infant primates (who unlike puppies and kittens are not normally reared in litters) do not appear to be able to interact with their peers before they are weaned, mobile, and able to use the communication systems unique to their species.

ROUGH-AND-TUMBLE PLAY

As they become more skilled in movement and communication, children become able to engage in what is called rough-and-tumble play. Rough and tumble is actually a shorthand term for a number of action patterns that are performed at a high pitch of activity, usually by a group. This type of play has been described by ethologists interested not only in play but in the total configuration of nursery-school activities. Typically, they observe a class or several classes over a period of time. Checklists of a variety of relatively simple, observable phenomena are prepared and defined as objectively as possible. The categories of these phenomena include facial expressions, vocalizations, postures and movements, aggressive behavior, other social gestures such as giving and showing. Items in the vocalization category, for example, usually include talk, scream, laugh, play noise, cry, sing. Other categories may specify the use of toys, equipment, and materials such as clay and paints. The age, sex, number of siblings, and length of nursery-school experience are usually noted for each child, and the time of day and the location (indoors or outdoors) may also be recorded. The raw data obtained are then analyzed first to determine how frequently the various items of behavior occur, what sorts of behavior cluster together in time, and then to relate these distributions of behavior to age, sex, school experience, and so forth.

From these accounts the cluster of activities called rough-and-tumble play has been identified. It is composed of run, hop, jump, fall over, chase, flee, wrestle, hit at, laugh, and make a face. It contrasts with aggressive conduct, which includes hit, push, take-tug-grab, stare down, and frown. Playfulness is signaled by laughter or making a play face, though exaggerated gestures or restraint in potentially violent movements probably also have communicative value. It is curious that there is so little information on the structure of children's rough-and-tumble play sequences as compared with the detailed accounts of cats and dogs provided by West, Bekoff, and others. We do not know how spontaneous bouts of chasing or mock fighting are conducted before organized and conventional playground games begin to appear. We do not know, for instance, what moves can start rough-and-tumble episodes, how longer sequences are built up, or how the bouts are usually concluded.

Studies conducted in England by Nicholas Blurton-Jones and by Peter Smith and Kevin Connolly provide the following picture of rough-and-tumble play at about four or five years of age.[10] It is more likely to occur out of doors and breaks out most spontaneously after children have just been released from a classroom or from set tasks. Compared with girls, boys engage in somewhat more vigorous activity with more noise and shouting and more close physical contact, such as wrestling and tumbling together. In a yard or designated play area, boys tend to move toward the periphery in larger mobile groups, and girls tend to play in a more restricted area, staying closer to the staff or playground equipment. Although girls also engage in rough and tumble, it is likely to be centered on slides or swings; and their groupings are smaller than those of boys.

In rough and tumble, as in other nursery-school activities, groups are usually made up of one sex. When other activities are taken into account, it appears that girls are attracted to more sedentary play with toys or art materials, tend to talk more with each other and spend more time with one or two partners. Boys race about more, make more and shorter social contacts, and focus less of their activity on toys and materials.

In general, younger children spend more time watching than engaging in boisterous play with others. Watching and observing may indeed be a form of exploration, and if so they would predictably precede spontaneous social play. However, even at about three years of age, children do take part in active social play, though they do so less often than older children. Their more cautious behavior may, in the groups observed, also reflect the fact that nursery school or other play group is a new experience for them. Observations of how new children are introduced and integrated into an existing nursery class show that it takes them some time to learn to interact with the more experienced children. For the neophytes, rough and tumble is the last activity they tend to engage in while getting acquainted with the veterans. It is also the case that first-born children spend more time watching and wandering about than do children with older siblings. These facts support the interpretation of rough and tumble as highly social and as different from intentional acts of aggression.

ROUGH AND TUMBLE IN OTHER CULTURES

The picture of rough and tumble in English and American nursery schools sketched above is probably widely valid. Boisterous, noisy, physical play in family, household, or village groups has been reported in diverse cultures, for example, among the Ilocano of Luzon, the Mixtecans of Mexico, and the Taira of Okinawa. It has been found that boys engage in more rowdy play than girls and that their groups move about more

and further away from adults. But even such natural, spontaneous activities as chasing and rough-housing are shaped by culture and environment. Among the Pilaga Indians and the !Kung
of Botswana, girls often engage in rough play. The !Kung boys
and girls play together; the Pilaga do too, but often with the
boys matched off against the girls. Pilaga girls from different vil-
lages conduct boxing bouts that appear violent, but in which
actual injury is not sanctioned.

The nature of a young child's social experience is of course related to community and family organization and to the child-
rearing practices of his society (for instance, time of weaning,
treatment of a child after the birth of a sibling, and time at which
responsibilities are assigned). In the non-Western and nonurban
cultures mentioned above, children in late infancy or early childhood spend much of their time in the care of older siblings and
often with other relatives or neighbors. If the households are isolated, the play groups are likely to be small, composed of mixed
ages and both sexes; if the dwellings are close together and the
community organization is open, then the groups are larger, but
still include a range of ages. Toys—articles made especially for
use by the young—are rare in all these communities and (with
the exception of the Mixtecans, who discourage group play for
girls) children are generally expected to play together. The Ny-
deggers wrote of the Ilocanos: "Just as adults are expected to
want companionship so the assumption is made with children. A
child playing alone must be lonely. The most striking thing
about children's play is that it is almost never solitary. Play
groups are encouraged if they are not voluntarily formed."[11] It
seems that because of this attitude toward sociability, because
each child is cared for by a number of others—some still children
themselves—and because he is exposed early to many other boys
and girls of various ages, active social play appears sooner in
these societies than in English and American nursery schools,
where many children encounter unfamiliar agemates for the first
time.

In most cultures, play with motion for its own sake is joined
with other aspects of play into more complex patterns. Rope
jumping conjoined with rhymed verses; chasing and fleeing
within a framework of social roles or themes such as Cops-and-
Robbers; and group or team activities that have specified rules,

limits, and sanctions, such as Hopscotch and Hide-and-Seek—all contain an action base of vigorous movement. In most human cultures play with motion does not disappear with approaching maturity, although it does come increasingly under the influence of social constraints and conventions that specify how, when, where, and by whom and in what garb the more boisterous and active types of play can be indulged.

4 / Play with Objects

Finding out what things are, how they work, and what to do with them occupies a great deal of the attention and efforts of the toddler and the young child. The term "toy" is often given to things that adults have designed or selected specifically to engage a child, but fascination with the properties of things extends to many other objects as well. It is perhaps this attractiveness of objects which has encouraged their widespread use as a research tool in the study of children's behavior, though they have an added advantage for the investigator in that they can be counted and their use described fairly objectively.

Objects serve as a link between the child and his environment in a number of ways. They provide a means by which a child can represent or express his feelings, concerns, or preoccupying interests. They also provide a channel for social interaction with adults or other children. Further, for the child an unfamiliar object tends to set up a chain of exploration, familiarization, and eventual understanding: an often-repeated sequence that will eventually lead to more mature conceptions of the properties (shape, texture, size) of the physical world.

Before examining play with objects, we can briefly review the immense achievements in the first year of life which make such play possible. Some of these accomplishments—the first step, the first word—are noted by parents. Other equally important achievements are seldom remarked, in part perhaps because they emerge gradually. For example, play with objects requires the achievement of visually directed grasping and adequate eye and hand coordination so that the child can pick up, hold, and turn objects. Such play further depends on the achievement of "object permanence," which is the understanding that an object continues to exist even though it is temporarily out of sight. It also requires some differentiation of action patterns, that is, the ability to perform different actions with an object. And building on the increasing voluntary control of physical movement, a baby develops the ability to repeat an action he has performed previously. More demanding still is the re-creation of an action someone else has performed—that is, imitation.

Imitation itself is a gradually emerging achievement that rests on both mental and physical development. The child first shows an ability to imitate certain actions he sees others perform; thereafter he will reproduce actions that he may have noticed several hours or even days before. This ability, called "delayed imitation," reflects the emerging capability to construct mental representations of actions and events, remember them, and be able to call them up even when the model is absent. At first this "memory" for actions is directly related to the physical sensations of performing the actions. At this time a child does not have verbal labels for action sequences or for objects, and his "concept" of an object is based on the sensory feedback of his experience with it. The object and his related action (patting a toy, opening a box) are therefore not separate phenomena. Jerome Bruner describes this mode of representing an action-object experience as the "enactive mode." Following this stage a child comes to make a distinction between the repeatable action pattern and the object or objects with which it was first linked. The nature of the child's representation of actions and their relations to objects next moves toward what Bruner has called the "iconic mode," the mode in which images or pictures of events and experiences organize the child's mental activities. Finally, as the child learns to associate the arbitrary and conventional labels of language with his own experiences, he moves into the "symbolic mode" of representation. He becomes able to symbolize an object or event with a word and gains yet another means for storing and retrieving aspects of his past experience. The symbolic mode of representation also enables him to use one object to represent another object. Thus the advent of symbolization ushers in the possibility of playing in a *qualitatively different way.*[1]

HOW OBJECT PLAY BEGINS

A composite picture of the changes that take place in a child's encounters with objects over the first three years can be drawn from the recent work of several psychologists. Although the procedures differed among the studies (for example, a child observed at home or a child seen in laboratory; limited sets of objects presented or a large group of objects presented), the trends toward more discriminating treatment of objects and greater complexity of object combinations are clear. In the following account, the ages are only approximate—individual children vary, some exhibiting a given type of behavior a bit earlier, some a bit later.

Several miniature objects—a cup, saucer, spoon, hairbrush, truck, trailer, doll—are placed before a child on a table. What is he likely to do? Following, in part, the work of Marianne Lowe,[2] we can predict that:

At *nine months*, the child will grasp a nearer, brighter object and bring it to his mouth; grasp another and do the same. After mouthing the object, he might well wave it or bang it on the table, then inspect it, turn it around, and bang it again or return it to his mouth. He uses only a few action patterns.

At *twelve months*, the child is likely to investigate (look at, turn, finger) each object *before* doing anything else with it. He might then put the spoon in his mouth once or twice, place it in the cup, and perhaps place the cup on the saucer, but other objects are still treated at random (mouthed, banged, waved).

At *fifteen months*, inspecting and investigating clearly precede other behavior. More and more consistently objects are accorded appropriate, or conventional, uses. The child will place the cup on the saucer and sip from it, and the spoon will be used more deliberately as if he were feeding himself. He will pick up the brush and run it over his hair; next he may push the truck back and forth. He may make the doll stand up.

At *twenty-one months*, the child will search for an object to "go with" other things. After putting the cup on the saucer, he will look for the spoon, find it, stir the imaginary drink and then drink it. He will then give the doll a drink from the cup or perhaps offer the observer a drink. He might brush his hair very carefully. He might place the doll in the truck.

At *twenty-four months*, the child feeds the doll realistically and lays it down for a nap after lunch. He brushes its hair and takes it for a ride in the truck. The truck and trailer will be lined up as if the truck were pulling the trailer, and the child may search for something to load into the trailer.

Between *thirty and thirty-six months*, the child will move the doll, making it pick up the cup and drink, then wash and dry the dishes, and put them away. The doll is made to brush its own hair. Thus the power to act purposefully is attributed to the doll. The truck and trailer are hooked together and moved with motor noises, and the doll may be made to drive the truck, perhaps to some specific location and back.

Over the two-year period these important developments stand out:

1. The child increasingly differentiates between various action patterns compatible with each object, and he fits together action and object appropriately (for example, he moves from mouthing every graspable object to putting only the spoon in his mouth).
2. He comes to combine objects that go together into functional relationships (he assembles the cup, saucer, and spoon).
3. He puts action patterns in sequence to form larger, coherent wholes (he links cooking, eating, and washing up).
4. He applies action patterns to himself (brushes his own hair), then to others or replicas of others (he brushes his mother's or a doll's hair). Finally, he attributes to replicas the ability to act (as when he causes the doll to brush its own hair or moves a toy dog while making barking noises).
5. He invents absent but appropriate objects or substances to complete action patterns (he stirs imaginary coffee with a toy spoon).
6. He transforms objects for use in actions and action sequences (he stirs imaginary coffee with a toy rake, used as a spoon).

These abilities are developed by acting on and interacting with the things and people around him. Their appearance through the second year of life indicates that the child is learning to play and beginning to engage in make-believe. But, more, these developments also reflect the beginnings of symbolic representation, a prerequisite to the development of language and abstract thinking. A progression from dependence on the physical properties of things to an ability to use signs that are completely arbitrary and conventional is well under way. The physical properties of things are taken as indications of their possible use, but they no longer solely determine that use. How exactly do these changes come about and how are they related? These are precisely the questions that are now being asked—and we still have no very full answers.

The manner in which the transformation of objects may develop has been suggested in the work of Greta Fein.[3] She presents a picture of orderly progression from single transformations to multiple ones. Fein tested forty-eight children between the ages of twenty-two and twenty-seven months to determine the conditions under which they would be able to use more and less realistic elements in a familiar action pattern; X eats from Y. These children were able to make a toy stuffed horse (X) eat from a plastic egg cup (Y). Most could also carry out the action with either a flat metal horse shape (X') and the egg cup (Y) or with the plush horse (X) and a shell (Y') for a food container. But when two substitutions were required at the same time (X' for X and Y' for Y, simultaneously), the children were not able to make the metal horse shape eat from the shell as if it were a dish or cup. Of course, even the toy horse and the egg cup, if they are combined in representing the action of eating, require transformation from a purely self-referenced experience of being fed or of feeding oneself. And to "feed the horse" one must treat the horse shape as if it were alive and the cup as if it contained food. But as the objects become more schematic, still further transformational steps are required. Fein's study suggests that learning to engage in symbolic play with objects progresses along a course from simple, single transformations to multiple and more complex ones. She concludes that in early make-believe activities an anchor (or realistic support) is required. Other studies have supported the notion that, when children first begin to play with objects, realistic replicas assist in their progress toward more imaginative deployment and combination of objects in pretend play. After a child has learned how to make believe, however, *less* realistic objects appear to facilitate make-believe play. They afford more scope for inventiveness and imagination, permitting the child to transform them to suit the occasion. Thus, for a skilled pretender, large cardboard boxes can be transformed into the family's home, the towers of a fort, a cave, cars on a freight train, or a witch's hut.

There is a paradox in the growth of pretending. As children become older, their use of objects in make-believe play becomes increasingly "appropriate." They represent more and more of the adult world in ways intelligible to us. The play becomes more realistic in that a greater range of details are provided, there are fewer idiosyncratic uses of objects and often greater faithfulness to the way things are in real life. At the same time, however, other details are treated quite cavalierly; there are often great flights of imagination and spur-of-the-moment invention. This paradox can be resolved in part when we look at a more advanced level of pretend play involving objects, a level typical of our three year old pairs. When a child is able to arrange utensils on a table, serve another child, tell him not to eat with his knife, and warn him that the food is very hot—all quite realistically—she may also appropriate the iron to serve as a teapot, if a proper one is missing. She will drastically abbreviate the time needed to cook a supper and will be quite happy to serve apple sauce from an empty pan. She may be oblivious to the fact that the dining table was, moments ago, the family car, or she may tell her partner to use a stuffed animal for a chair. Some aspects of this episode are only suggestive or schematic, as Lowe also observed in her subjects at three. It appears that the complex action plan, here the notion of serving and dining, has become more important than the objects themselves.

FROM DISCOVERY AND EXPLORATION TO EXPLOITATION AND PLAY

What happens when a young child encounters an object that is new to him? Will he begin straight away to play with it? Most usually he will not. There is, instead, a progression from discovery and simple manipulation to imaginative use of objects.

It is obviously not easy to cut up what may occur as a continuous flow of activity, but certain distinctions can be made according to the degree to which unrestrained and spontaneous play predominates. Listed in order of increasing adaptation to an object or experience are (a) exploration, (b) manipulation, (c) practice, and (d) repetition, with or without imaginative elaboration. Some of these terms have also been applied to aspects of play other than use of objects, but the following example will illustrate how these four types of orientation appeared in succession in one child's encounter with an object that was new to him. A three-year-old boy saw a large wooden car in our playroom for the first time. (a) He paused, inspected it, and touched it. (b) He then tried to find out what it could do. He turned the steering wheel, felt the license plate, looked for a horn, and tried to get on the car. (c) Having figured out what the object was and what it could do, he got to work on what *he* could do with *it*. He put telephones on it, took them off, next put cups and dishes on it. These activities were a form of trying out ideas to see how they would work. Finally, the car was understood, its properties and immediate usefulness reasonably clear. (d) He then climbed on it and drove furiously back and forth with suitable motor and horn noises. We can readily accept the last activity as play. The activities that led up to the last incident, however, seem less playful. Though (a), (b), and (c) do not seem quite like hard work, they do suggest a process of continuous testing and of learning what the object is and how it might be treated.

An important study by Corinne Hutt was designed specifically to disentangle the characteristics of exploration from those of play.[4] She constructed a novel object—a box with a movable lever to which four visible counters, a buzzer, and a bell were connected. Movements of the lever were recorded by the counters. Depending on how the object was preset, moving the lever could produce four different effects: (a) bell and buzzer sounding, counters visible; (b) bell and buzzer sounding, counters covered; (c) bell and buzzer off, counters visible; (d) bell and buzzer off, counters covered. Nursery-school children, aged three to five, were brought individually to a familiar room containing the box and five more conventional toys. Each child had six ten-minute sessions with the object. The children would approach it, inspect it, and then begin to manipulate the lever. They soon tired of the box when moving the lever produced no effects (d), and even with a view of the moving counters (c) their attention flagged by the third session. Producing noises with the bell and buzzer (b) kept them actively occupied through the fifth session. Addition of the visible counters to the sound effects, however, elicited the most extensive manipulation of the lever. The complexity of the results obtained from working the lever, and particularly the sound of bell and buzzer, promoted and increased active contact with the object.

Hutt also observed distinct differences between investigative-exploratory behavior and certain other types of behavior that were directed to the novel object. The former were characterized by full attention, facing and looking directly toward the object, cautiously feeling and touching it. The latter included many more diverse activities, which were actually of two types. One kind included repetitive movements (like patting the lever over and over again), continuous handling without looking at it directly (leaning on the lever to give a continuous ring while looking around the room), and subordinating the object to some other action plan (for instance, racing around the room carrying a truck and ringing the bell at each pass). The other kind Hutt called "transposition-function"; the child used the object for some other purpose (perhaps climbed on it, walked over it, or sat on it). The illustrations here very clearly show the contrasts between the concentration of exploration and the nonchalance and enjoyment of play.

The processes of exploration and familiarization, which must precede play with novel objects, new settings, unfamiliar events or unknown persons, are obviously associated with learning—that is, developing new conceptualizations for dealing with parts of the world. But perhaps play also contributes to learning in some way. Although the properties of an object (what it is, what it can do) may be known to some extent, new possibilities for its use or its potentiality for combination may be discovered in the course of playing with it. By definition, such learning would be "incidental" since the term "play" is restricted to activity that lacks any extrinsic goal. Still, the play orientation might conceivably facilitate what we would call creativity and what some psychologists have named divergent thinking.* The possibility that a playful orientation promotes insight into solutions of problems or that a playful orientation is characteristic of creativ-

*Divergent thinkers are good at flights of imagination, as in dreaming up the most, and also the most original, uses for a simple object. Convergent thinkers tend to arrive at more conventional solutions in an orderly way. We all use convergent and divergent thinking, though some people are more strongly disposed to one or the other style.

Characteristic patterns of exploring a novel object

ity has motivated a good deal of research. Obviously these possibilities have important implications for educational practices as well as for an understanding of how scientific discoveries and artistic innovations come about.

CREATIVE PROBLEM SOLVING AND OBJECT PLAY

It may now be clearer why a more precise distinction between exploration and play is important. What is the relationship between play and innovative or successful problem solving? Phrased more generally, does play promote creative thinking?

Kathy Sylva has attempted to distinguish between the effects of manipulating and becoming familiar with objects and the effects of prior playful, imaginative behavior involving the objects later used as tools in the solution of a task.[5] Sylva asked middle-class children from a day-care center to get a piece of chalk out of a plastic box that opened on release of a simple latch. The box was out of reach of hand and could not be touched by either of two sticks that were provided along with two clamps. The solution to the problem was to clamp the sticks together, flip up the latch with the extended stick, and rake the chalk out. Several different experimental conditions preceded the children's attempts at solution. In one experiment, some children watched an adult construct the tool; others were permitted to handle the tools freely and play with them if they liked. In another experiment some children watched an adult dramatize the construction of the tool by animating "Mr. Clamp," who put his teeth around the sticks. Still other children were given specific training in how to construct the tool. Regardless of their experience prior to the attempted solution, all children were given standardized hints if they did not proceed by themselves to the solution. The prior experience of freely handling the sticks and clamps was just as effective as watching an adult demonstrate the correct combination. Prior free handling, however, also led to more subsequent activity directed to the ultimate goal of obtaining the chalk; to somewhat more systematic, step-by-step procedures; and to more effective use of the hints, if hints had been given. Surprisingly, watching the amusing dramatization and receiving training were both relatively ineffective. Sylva concluded that free handling was more effective because only then did the children initiate the solution themselves. They had had the opportunity to explore alternative steps in the process and had also gained, perhaps, a more relaxed attitude toward the task.

But how do we know that the free handling was play? It could have been exploration or manipulation lacking any playful orientation to the objects. Sylva reexamined the behavior and success of those children who had the prior experience of handling the objects and found that a majority of them had actually played; they had engaged in some transformation of the materials, such as shaping a house or forming a letter A. The "transformers" were the children whose problem-solving performances were most efficient and effective. Thus, although it is not correct to say that playing *caused* better problem solving, it is true that those children who displayed nonliteral or imaginative behavior prior to the task were the best problem solvers.

THE ROLE OF OBJECTS IN SOCIAL CONTACTS

Objects are the prime currency of social exchange for the toddler. Through the second year of life, showing, sharing, giving, retrieving, and appropriating are the most frequent bases for his voluntary interactions with adults and other children. Newly mobile infants observed on a park outing with their mothers would quickly move away from the mother. When they encountered some arresting object, they would either turn to the mother and point to it while looking directly at her or, if the object was portable, bring it back for her inspection. In situations of more controlled observation children of twelve to eighteen months have been shown to bring or show adults (parent or observer) what they find interesting, and to do so often and continuously.

From twice-weekly observations of a play group of toddlers, Edward Mueller noted that virtually the only concerted action of the five otherwise independent members of the group followed on "discovery" of some object.[6] For example, when one child accidentally caused the bell of a train to ring, all the children gathered around the train to touch or try to ring the bell. A common focus of attention sustained an episode of parallel play. As Mueller put it, "The children did not interact with one another, so much as they unilaterally and simultaneously acted upon a common object." He found, however, that later in the three-month observation period two children's joint object-centered behavior sometimes changed into more person-centered interactions. Initially drawn to the train Loren was pulling, Robert began to follow Loren and then to imitate the course and direction of Loren's movements. At this point Loren became interested in Robert's running. Alternating rounds of lead and follow, with "happy-sounding cries and screams," grew out of Robert's initial pursuit of the object. Direct involvement with the same toy has been widely observed to be the most common basis for child-related behavior in groups of two-year-olds. Among somewhat older children, objects are still an important part of social exchanges. The Waterhouses in their study of English nursery classes observed that a newcomer to the class was first contacted with "gifts."[7] Toys, sweets, or personal belongings were offered in the overtures to friendship.

Showing a familiar object to a new adult or a new object to a familiar adult appears in itself to be one of the basic forms of communication for very young children. But the vocalizing that generally accompanies showing begins to stabilize to fairly consistent signals. One infant may use Ha! Ha!, another Eee! to accompany pointing, but each may use quite a different signal when giving. Most adults are responsive to these physical gestures, which are easily interpreted as sharing. The adults predictably respond with some type of recognition by looking, smiling, reaching, and often by saying Thank you or Isn't that pretty? Thus, not only does the object serve as a vehicle for communication, but sharing objects is one of the first events in which verbal communication becomes closely linked to a specific action performed by a child in a social situation.

Of course, objects have another, powerful attraction: they can be possessed. The short- or long-term association of person and object is one of the earliest concepts encoded in speech and appears in unambiguous form by the time the child can form two-word utterances. From that time at least, but probably even before speech, possession is an important notion. I was once introduced to a two-year-old and said, "Hello, Betsy. How are you?" "Mine," she responded firmly, holding out a coloring book.

A number of studies of nursery-school groups and of pairs of mothers and children in laboratory playrooms have implicated objects as the focus not only of cooperation and pleasant reciprocal exchanges but also of contention and physical struggle. Ownership or even temporary possession of an object by another child makes that object doubly interesting. Carol Eckerman noted that for two-year-olds "a toy on the ground does not equal a toy in the hand of a peer."[8] Contentions most usually involve a struggle over objects. Just taking or attempting to take an object from another child, however, is not necessarily an aggressive move on the part of a toddler. That is, such an action may not actually be "intended" as hurtful. Often the child who reaches out to appropriate another's toy is clearly taken aback and surprised when the owner howls or struggles.

Assignment of possession was a major focus of conversation between several pairs of three-year-olds in our paired agemate sessions. The discussions were usually pursued quite solemnly and harmoniously. One instance concerned a dress-up hat found in a box: A: *Is this yours?* B: *No.* A: *It's mine?* B: *Yes.* A: *It's mine?* B: *Sure it is.* Equitable distribution of objects for some other purpose was also an absorbing activity. Several pairs became so engrossed with apportioning props for a tea party that the party itself was forgotten: A: *You get a knife and I get a knife.* B: *Here's a cup for me and a cup for you.* A: *Where's my saucer?* B: *Here's a blue saucer for you and the green one is for me,* and so on and on until every item had been allocated.

Play with objects has important links with social development. Reflection on our own earliest childhood memories, however, may reveal that certain objects had strong private emotional appeal. Many people's earliest and most vivid recollections are of some toy. My own are of almost perfect tiny replicas of a table service complete with a fat, brown roast turkey on a platter, red cranberry sauce, vegetables, and a centerpiece of flowers, all part of the furnishings of a doll's house. The powerful emotional appeal of direct experience with objects is captured by the novelist John Updike, writing in *Women and Museums* of childhood visits to a museum where he was entranced by several small bronze figures: "They were in their smallness like secret thoughts of mine projected into dimension and permanence, and they returned to me as a response that carved strangely into parts of my body."

TOY PREFERENCES

The fact that children are attracted to certain kinds of toys along sex-appropriate lines is well known, and some psychologists have considered toy preference as indicative of the child's own sexual identification. Boys consistently choose "masculine" kinds of toys such as soldiers or trucks. Although girls tend to choose dolls and household objects, their interests are generally more versatile. Girls also choose masculine toys, though less consistently than boys do. The origins of these preferences can be traced in large part to parental behavior, to the parents' influence as models and to their approval or support of children's interest in sex-stereotyped objects. A very striking example of even more direct parental control of children's early exposure to types of toys is provided by a study of the private rooms of ninety-six children of upper-middle-class families, in age from under one to six.[9] There was no great difference between the boys' and girls' rooms in respect to the presence of books, furniture, musical objects, and stuffed animals. Boys had more varieties of objects than girls did. The boys' rooms contained far more toy animals in barns or zoos, objects relating to space, matter, energy, or time (magnets, puzzles, space ships). The girls' rooms contained more dolls, floral designs on wallpaper and fabrics, and ruffles or lace. Even though boys' rooms contained some dolls (for instance, cowboys), virtually none represented females or babies.

The most extreme difference was in the number of vehicles owned by the boys (375) as compared to the girls (17). No girl at any age had a wagon, bus, motorcycle, boat, or trailer. The typical boy of two had at least three vehicles and by the age of three the average was eleven. Further, only boys had live animals, depots, replicas of heavy equipment, and military toys; only girls had doll's houses, stoves, tea sets, and cradles for dolls. Harriet Rheingold, who directed this study, observes that in her laboratory girls of eighteen months spent as much time playing with trucks as boys did. She concludes that parents were not acceding to the spontaneous interests of their children but were themselves primarily responsible for the extremely different inventories of objects found in the boys' and girls' private rooms. The high-level socioeconomic class in this study might be expected to be less extreme in regard to sex stereotyping than the general population, so that this difference in the toys given to boys and girls is probably quite widespread. Certainly the sex preferences in toys in freely chosen activities in nursery schools, which Margaret Parten remarked on in 1933, are still in evidence today.[10] Boys cluster at the tool bench or push trucks around the room, and girls gather in the kitchen corner to cook and wash dishes in most of the free-activity periods we have observed.

EXPRESSIVE BEHAVIOR WITH OBJECTS

In their play with dolls and other objects children sometimes appear to associate the dolls with members of their own families and will almost always choose a same-sex doll to represent themselves. Children may portray events they themselves have experienced and represent situations that presumably have some importance for them. Objects are thus incorporated into the child's expressive behavior. These expressive aspects have led to clinical and therapeutic applications of the child's treatment of dolls and other toys. I will not go into play therapy except to note that therapists generally stress its cathartic aspects. They stress the notion that, by representing a traumatic experience or situation symbolically and by returning to it and perhaps reversing its outcome in play, the child becomes better able to deal with the problem in his real life. One of the values of play for therapy has been stated by Erik Erikson: "That the metaphoric expression of intimate experiences in free play 'loosens' the communicability of these same experiences is, of course, the main rationale of play therapy."[11]

Doll play with a restricted inventory of realistically constructed human figures has been widely used to study aggression, racial prejudice, parent preference, and attitudes toward siblings. Anthropologists Jules and Zunia Henry employed a typical procedure to study sibling rivalry among Pilaga Indian children in Argentina.[12] These children are abruptly displaced at the birth of a sibling and ignored by parents and relatives, who turn all their attention to the new infant. The rejected children were given realistic dolls matched in sex, age, and number to members of their own family. Though unaccustomed to realistic dolls (their own were crudely formed of bone and clay), the children played with the new dolls in their normal fashion, representing familiar but impersonal and stereotyped village and family activities. When the Henrys named the new dolls for the children and members of their family, however, the play became more personal. The children manipulated the self-doll and the others to symbolize hostility (kicking and biting). The dramatized aggression was directed at parents and siblings, and even toward themselves. The children also depicted the self-doll as nursing, which the Henrys interpreted as indicating a desire to return to their former, more favored status as infants.

Caution is necessary in drawing inferences about a child's attitudes, emotions, or previous experiences from his choice or treatment of objects. Two qualifications must be taken into account. First, even a child is aware that there is an important difference between depicting an event through objects or props and actually experiencing that event. It is true that at times the child appears to forget these facts when he is playing, but play generally reflects a *willing* suspension of disbelief. Second, treatment of objects in play is not actually realistic. Although some behavior is copied faithfully from a model, some is only roughly suggestive of events in the nonplay world. The child does select those aspects of experience that matter most to him, but there is also an element of convention or stylization in the depictions of his experience. Further, the child can combine both remembered and imagined events, mixing into one sequence material from a bedtime story, memories of actual events, an image from a television program, a frustrated impulse, a scene witnessed in another child's home, and a stereotyped association of objects and people or of objects and acts that he has learned in a previous play episode with friends.

If these cautions are kept in mind, then children's attraction to objects and replicas and their willingness and ability to depict events by manipulating toys can be used to learn from the child what he is not able to convey directly or succinctly in conversations or interviews with an adult. Although I will discuss this topic more extensively in Chapter Six, it is appropriate here to describe briefly a very interesting use of object play as a research technique. Sidney Brower and some associates are designing play spaces for children in lower socioeconomic neighborhoods in a crowded urban area in the United States. They have brought together pairs of elementary-school classmates, including some aged six, and have presented them with a schematic, scaled-down model of a typical area with streets, alleys, sidewalks, houses, and small backyards. The children are given a few cars and several parent and child dolls. The behavior that results (with very little prompting and only a few suggestions, such as *Show us your favorite games*) is videotaped. Amazingly fluent representations of sidewalk and street games, car accidents and their consequences, and other important and exciting events have been obtained. The parent dolls warn against the dangers of the street; a game of Dodge Ball or Hide-and-Seek is conducted in great detail; a group of boys ventures into another neighborhood and is chased off by bigger boys and their dogs. There are dramatic exaggerations and elements of fantasy, but certain themes and incidents recur among different pairs of children. Gradually a composite picture of the patterns of activities and use of spaces characteristic of these children emerges; and this picture can be checked with first-hand observations and with interviews and reports as well. This information can then be used in designing play spaces compatible with the needs and interests of the children and the neighborhoods.

Throughout childhood, play with objects undergoes many changes. As the child becomes more skilled and experienced, his playful treatment of objects becomes more diverse and sophisticated. Both imagination and intellectual curiosity begin to contribute to his play—paper dolls are clad in colorful and detailed costumes; intricate constructions are built from modeling sets or sand. More and more, meaningful associations accrue to objects, and play with objects is combined with other aspects of play. Often, as we will see in later chapters, objects are incorporated as props in dramatic play, or their treatment is governed by complex rules in games of physical or intellectual skill. All through these changes, however, objects continue to arouse curiosity and the desire to learn. They provide enjoyment in mastering their use or in understanding the properties of things, and they also continue to facilitate social contacts and to assist in the expression of ideas and feelings.

5 / Play with Language

The use of newly acquired resources for playful exploitation is most striking in children's play with language. Almost all the levels of organization of language (phonology, grammar, meaning) and most phenomena of speech and talking, such as expressive noises, variation in timing and intensity, the distribution of talk between participants, the objectives of speech (what we try to accomplish by speaking) are potential resources for play. It is curious that there has been little systematic study of this topic, since play with language and speech provides overt and easily observable forms of behavior. But this behavior is rather difficult to quantify (a score of one for a pun? two for a rhyme?), and it is of course difficult to elicit in experimental studies. There are, however, a few excellent collections based on anecdotes or informal observations, and these suggest that the child from two to six is fascinated with the resources of language and that he is sensitive to the play potential in this newly discovered world.

The Russian writer of verses and stories for children, Kornei Chukovsky, sees in this period a time of verbal creativity when the newcomer to the world of linguistic sounds and symbols brings a fresh eye to the marvels of language.[1] Unlike the adult who is sated with the sounds and metaphoric nature of everyday language, the child finds word shapes and the figurative properties of meaning a source of delight. Chukovsky quotes a four-year-old who raced to the table with the original demand: *Give me, give me, before I die, lots and lots of potato pie.* Children's questions often reveal surprising insight into the meaning structure of language, as these queries indicate: Couldn't table legs be fitted with shoes? Since there is running water, is there sitting water? Did the man really leave town under a cloud? It is important to note that at least some of the child's "errors" in building new words are often a result of productive linguistic rules for word formation. He can create verbs from nouns—*I am blocking* (building a tower with blocks)—and he can create nouns from verbs—*Look! A sweep!* (on discovering a toy broom).

Extensive collections of jump-rope rhymes and songs, charms and chants, jokes and other verbal accompaniments to play activities have also been made, most notably by Iona and Peter Opie.[2] Other collections confirm their findings of a powerful and long-standing oral tradition of play with language in the folk cultures of school-age children. The Opies stress the historical and geographic continuity of form and function of these materials and suggest a direct transmission from child to child rather than adult-mediated diffusion. The reader probably remembers, for example, if he ever learned Pig Latin, that his instructor was not a parent but another child.

In this chapter we will be primarily concerned not with codified songs and rhymes or with traditional incantations, verbal jokes, and insults (*See my thumb? Boy, you're dumb!*) but with the more ephemeral productions of play with language. We will examine the unrehearsed use of linguistic resources for fun, first looking at verbal play with noises and sounds, then at the different linguistic levels of phonology, grammatical forms, and meaning, and finally at play with the pragmatic or functional aspects of conversation.

In our agemate sessions most of the play with language or speech was spontaneously generated rather than quoted. An exception was a fragment of a nursery rhyme produced as a descriptive comment. A girl of five saw that a doll was missing a shoe and ran off the lines, *One shoe off and one shoe on. Diddle diddle dumpkin my son John.* She and her partner smiled at this apt quotation, but no further play resulted. Of the few cases in which lines from traditional verses or tunes were repeated, most were solitary performances and only rarely did they become a basis for a joint production. We do not know why the songs and rhymes of nursery school and home were so rarely reflected in these sessions, but it is noteworthy that very little play was based directly on nursery school experiences such as games or class expeditions.

PLAY WITH NOISES AND SOUNDS

The most primitive level at which verbal play is conducted is that of articulation or phonation—the actual process of making sounds. In the babbling stage, usually at its peak between six and ten months, the child produces a great variety of sounds. These random noises, however, are not the immediate precursors of the vowels and consonants of language. Many disappear from the repertoire altogether, and others have little resemblance to the units of the phonological system which are later represented in the meaningful words of the language. Vocalizing does continue through the early periods of language acquisition but tends to appear only in noncommunicative settings. Recordings of solitary one-year-olds show long episodes of vocal modulation of a single vowel, with the voice melodically rising and falling, varied with other sound effects such as a quavering voice. Stable syllabic forms are also repeated at great length (for example, *Ba, Ba, Ba*), with or without minor vowel or consonant modifications. When the child does begin to talk (the first intelligible word is usually reported at about ten months to a year) and learns to produce and control the contrast between making vocal noises and speaking, it is then possible to identify episodes of verbal play with sound.

Repetitive, rhythmic vocalizations are associated with pleasurable states in the prelinguistic child, and infant-parent games very often include a vocal component. The parent's "swelling" oooh-sound of mock threats and loomings, the popping noises and tongue clicking that accompany tickling, finger-walking, or jiggling, are among the first models of vocal play the infant encounters. His own use of playful vocalizations continues as he learns to talk and, through the preschool period, becomes increasingly differentiated from other uses of speaking.

Syllable shapes and prosodic features such as intonation and stress provide the raw material for early language play. Controlled variation in articulation, such as rasping, whispering, or nasalization, are also favorite materials. Making noises can be enjoyed as absorbing in itself or can be used to provide special sound effects (such as engine noises). With strict regulation of tempo, vocal noises can provide rhythmic accompaniment for play with motion (humming or tongue clicking while hopping or banging some object).

Vocalizations as accompaniments to movement grow from hums, squeals, and bellowings to repetitive, often melodic strings of syllables. Music to iron a fish by was provided by a boy of three. The syllables *dá: ti, dá: ti** initiated the chant and were gradually varied in a loose singsong rhythm. Vowels provided the main source of variation. The sequence was:

> Da ti di
> da ti di
> da ti di
> da da da
> do di da
> do di da
> di do da di go bo di
> di do da di go bo di
> di do da di go bo di

The boy's partner did not join in this chant.

Sequences of nonsense syllables move to chants built on recognizable word shapes with fairly regular patterns of stress and pitch. But in all these types of playful vocalization the meaning of the words is secondary or nonexistent, and it is only the sound and rhythm that are enjoyed or that enhance the accompanying activity. Harriet Johnson provides an example of a chant produced by a two-and-a-half-year-old upon completing a block-building project.[3]

> Now it's dóne un ún
> Dóne un ún un ún

Between the ages of two and three an important advance takes place. Conventionalized noises are learned and used to identify certain events and actions. These noises, each of which has a specific meaning, appear to be an almost essential part of the particular event or action. Moreover, insofar as they are conventional, the noises can also identify the meaning of what is

---

*A colon after a vowel symbol indicates lengthening. When it is pertinent to the discussion, relative stress, or loudness, is marked *directly over* a vowel by ´ (primary stress and ˋ (secondary stress); unstressed syllables are unmarked.

happening for a playmate. Some of these noises are built from the sound units (phonemes) of the child's language, but others represent noises that do not occur in the formation of English words.

Examples of such action-identifying tags used by American children are: ding-a-ling (telephone), ruff-ruff (dog barking), tyap-tyap or nyam-nyam (sound of eating), pow-pow (explosions of a gun). Beep-beep is an automobile horn, and the racing-engine sound could be written as vroom-vroom, though that sound is much more complex than the spelling suggests.* Exact repetition of a syllable is the characteristic means of formation for most of the tags. They are used to fill in or elaborate the context of pretending and always accompany the appropriate physical activity.

Distortion of normal articulation over a whole utterance is another way in which vocal capabilities can be played with. Several pairs in our group engaged in "talking funny." For example, trying to speak with the lips held spread wide and rigid or talking in a squeaky or gruff voice was a source of amusement in itself and could be shared by both. Just talking funny is somewhat different from changing the voice to signal an adopted identity, such as infant, father, baby fish, in episodes of make-believe with role enactment (see Chapter Eight). In the latter cases various aspects of speaking are used to mark an assumed role and to express pretend attitudes, but are not themselves the major focus of play.

Solitary singing or humming can be related thematically to some concurrent action, as was the chant *Now it's done un un.* But the song or chant can itself become a primary focus of attention, continuing beyond the action that triggered it off. For example, a boy (2:10) picked up a toy dunebuggy (named for him by one of the observers, who then left the room). First the word *dunebuggy* was explored for its syllabic possibilities, and the stress pattern was adjusted (*dúnebùggy → dúne bú-ggý*); next

---

*It is interesting that some of these forms involve sounds that do not occur in the phonological system employed in normal speech. *Vroom-vroom*, for example, uses a type of r-sound that is not a component of English phonology. Such sounds prove very difficult for adults attempting to learn foreign languages that do systematically employ the sounds.

the initial consonant was modified (*dune* —→ *june*) and the first syllable duplicated (*júne júne bú-ggý*); finally to the four approximately equally stressed syllables was added a rhythmic contour with slight terminal pitch rise. Throughout the three-minute sequence, the child walked about and casually examined a large wooden car and a stool with a magnifying glass in the center. The chant itself had become the focal activity while the object that triggered it was quite forgotten.

The preceding example utilizes sound for play, but the sounds are more clearly linguistic elements and the intonational features are similar if not identical to the prosodic features of pitch and stress that are part of the phonological system of communicative speech. Thus this example appears to be transitional between play with noises and sound and play with features of the linguistic system.

Playing with sounds and noises appears to be primarily a private activity. Only one report of social play with nonsense syllables has been published so far. Elinor Keenan videotaped her twins (2:10) during the first hours of a morning when they were alone.[4] She obtained a wide variety of joint, well-synchronized linguistic play activities (songs, poems, ritual insults) as well as instances of sound play, which she defined as "utterances which cannot be referentially interpreted by an adult native speaker." Some of these employed possible English syllables, but many included sounds or processes that are not part of the English phonological system. Since our pair sessions contained no such joint performances, it may be that only children who are very well acquainted can produce structured verbal play as in this excerpt from Keenan's twins:

Child 1	*Child 2*
(1) apshi: autshi: apshi: autshi: o:tshi: o:shabatsh	
	(2) sha: shabatsh:
(3) sho:babatsh	
	(4) sho:babat shobabatsh (laugh)
(5) sho:bababatsh	

PLAY WITH THE LINGUISTIC SYSTEM

The period from two to three is one of rapid linguistic achievement. Playful use of language at this time has been reported, though primarily for solitary children. The most detailed account is that by Ruth Weir, who recorded the presleep monologues of her son Anthony (2:10).[5] These recordings revealed the seemingly indefatigable practice of linguistic structures. Anthony experimented with the phonological properties of nonsense syllables and words: *Let Bobo bink. Bink ben bink. Blue kink.* He systematically substituted words of the same grammatical categories: *What color mop. What color glass.* He built up and broke down sentences, thus isolating their components: *Stop it. Stop the ball,* and *Anthony jump out again. Anthony jump.* He exercised conversational exchanges, often asking and answering questions, congratulating or warning himself, and he practiced counting, listing, and naming. His paragraphs, defined by Weir as sequences of utterances chained by phonological, grammatical, or semantic links, often show the simultaneous use of these links:

Anthony's speech	*Weir's comments*
That's office. That's office.	Sound play with the
Look Sophie.	pronunciation of *That's office*
That Sophie.	and *Sophie,* with substitution
Come last night.	in the sentence frame. Break-
Good boy.	ing down a complete sentence.
Go for glasses.	Recall of recent event and
Go for them.	self-congratulations on keeping
Go to the top.	hands off forbidden glasses.
Go throw . . . etc.	More systematic substitution in
	frame. Rhyming phrase.

It is likely that many children, when they are alone, conduct similar bouts of playful language exploration, which has been called practice play. In the reported cases of solitary monologuing the speech differs in a number of ways from the child's speech produced in conversations with a goal, as when he wishes to influence another person's actions. In private linguistic excursions the child becomes aware of the structural properties of his language and increasingly skilled in the fluent production of normal speech. He experiments with the componential structure of sentences as well as with their prosodic possibilities. In fact, he playfully takes apart and puts together building blocks of sequences that he cannot until several years later consciously isolate or decompose. Even at the beginning of elementary school, children cannot segment a word into syllables or identify the word boundaries in utterances when asked to do so. There is evidence, however, that children vary considerably in the degree to which they engage in such solitary practice with their newly acquired linguistic abilities, and we do not yet know whether practice play with language is essential to normal language development.

In social interactions among children, the distinction between such exploration of linguistic structure and play with language is somewhat clearer. First, each partner must know whether what the other has said requires a playful or nonplayful response, and thus the productions are distinctly marked as playful, if they are so intended. Second, the pressures of responsive communication do not permit the lengthy and leisurely unfolding of private meaning associations or privately intriguing sound variations, such as those Anthony pursued. Keenan's twins at 2:10 years did jointly produce, in alternating turns, sequences of nonsense syllables as well as intelligible phrases with rhymes and phonological variations that were very similar to Anthony's linguistic exercises. But in our pairs of acquainted and unacquainted children, play with language resources was rarely shared with a partner until after three. And then the interactive play with language tended to be repetitive and predictably structured—that is, less like a stream of associations and more like a measured, alternating current. However, from about three and a half virtually all levels of language structure were used as a basis for social play.

From this point on, we will examine social play with language as conducted in the pair sessions. In that setting, of course, the children could be socially engaged or could ignore one another altogether. When not engaged, one or both children sometimes produced private speech that was somewhat similar to Anthony's solitary performances; one example is the manipulation of the word *dunebuggy*. They made up chants and explored word shapes, but indulged in few grammatical buildups, breakdowns, and substitutions. One girl (3:4) in an unacquainted pair tried to engage her partner in a conversation. Failing to get a response she conducted a dialogue herself with an imaginary Mr. Smugla, which began:

> Smugla, Mr. Smugla I can't bring my daughter.
> Why? Why? Why? Why?
> She didn't have any dresses—or shirts or pants.
> Then I'll keep her in her pyjamas.
> But she can't stay in them.

This continued for four minutes.

It may be that the very presence of another child, no matter how uncooperative, leads another child toward forms of language play that are less "analytical" and more like normal conversation.

SOCIAL PLAY

We can distinguish three types of social play with language: spontaneous rhyming and word play; play with fantasy and nonsense; and play with speech acts and discourse conventions. More than one type can be represented in a single interactive episode, but it appears that the distinctions have to do with some basically different uses of language resources for play.

Spontaneous rhyming and word play. Spontaneous social word play arose in our pair sessions from interactions already in progress, most commonly from states of mutual attending and desultory conversation. It did not tend to arise in more mutually absorbing states such as pretending or in goal-oriented episodes such as trying to fix a broken toy or arguing about something.

The most obvious type of word play is rhyme. Children's predilection for rhythm, rhyme, and alliteration is well known. Only a few simple rhymes were constructed by our sample of children. In the following instance, one child was responsible for the rhyme *high/sky*; the other repeated the leader's words and rhythm but concluded the sequence with a sincere request for information.

Boy (4:1)	Boy (3:9)
(handles small ladder and pipe)	(watches)
(1) I need `this.	
	(2) You need `that.
(3) You go ´way up` high.	
	(4) You go ´way up` high.
(5) You go ´high in the` sky. Nobody can ˎsee.	
	(6) Nobody can ´see?
	(7) Nobody can ´see?
(8) ˎYeah.	

A single word utterance provided a rhyming exchange for another pair: *sparky/darky*. However, only an older, previously acquainted pair produced a multiple exchange containing a sequence of rhymes and variations on word shape and prosodic features.

Boy (5:2)	Girl (5:4)
(both children simultaneously wander and handle various objects, little direct gaze)	
(1) And when Melanie and . . . and you will be in here you have to be `grand`mother ´grand ˎmother. ´Right?*	
	(2) I'll have to be ˎgrand ´momma ˎgrand´ momma ˋgrand ˎmomma. (in distorted voice)
(3) ˎGrand⌢mother grand⌃ mother ˎgrand ˎmother.	
	(4) ˎGrand⌢momma ˎgrand ˎmomma ˎgrand ˎmomma.
(5) ˎGrand⌢mother ˎgrand ˎmother ˎgrand ˎmother.	
	(6) ˎGrand⌢momma ˎgrand ˎmother ˎgrand ˎmomma.
(7) ⌃Momma.	
	(8) ⌃Momma´I . . . . my ˎmommy ˎmomma.

*For a reminder about pitch markings, see the note on page 13.

(10) ˋHey.

(laugh)

(13) ˋPeer.

(15) ˏPooper.

(17) ˏPooper. Now ˋthat's a . . .
ˋthat's a good ˏname.

(9) ˏMother ˏhumpf.

(11) ˋMother ˋmear (laugh)
ˋmother ˋsmear.

(12) I said ˋmother ˋsmear
ˏmother ˏnear ˏmother ˏtear
ˋmother ˋdear. (laugh)

(14) ˋFear.

(16) ´What?

The stress and pitch possibilities and the common lexical variations (*mother, momma, mommy*) were fairly well exhausted by
this pair.

The sounds of words appear to be more available for spontaneous play than their grammatical shape. A common process
for forming diminutives is the addition of /iː/, spelled *y* or *ie*, to
the last consonant of a monosyllable (*doggie*) or to a nonfinal
consonant of a polysyllabic word (*Kathy* or *Robbie*). A formally
similar process changes a noun to an adjective that means "having the quality of the noun" (*fishy, rainy*). These were the only
grammatical operations the children played with. The first process, along with duplication of the word, is illustrated by the following exchange (all the words relate to toys and objects in our
observation room):

Boy (5:2)

(inspects stuffed animals)
(1) ˋTeddy bear's⌢mine.

(3) No, the ˋsnakey⌢snakey is
ˏyours.

Girl (5:7)

(busy with suitcase)

(2) The ˋfishy´fishy is⌢mine.

The adjective-forming process was used as the basis for a sophisticated exchange of pure word play:

Boy (5:7)	*Girl* (5:2)
(wandering)	(moving ironing board)
(1) 'Cause it's fishy too.	
(2) 'Cause it has fishes.	
	(3) And it's snakey too 'cause it has snakes and it's beary too because it has bears.
(4) And it's . . . and it's hatty 'cause it has hats.	

Play with fantasy and nonsense.   Nonsense and verse, with or without rhyme, and nonsense stories add a dimension of meaning or meaning distortion as a resource for play. Nonsense verse and topsy-turvy meanings appeal to children of our age range. Chukovsky wrote, "Hardly has the child comprehended with certainty which objects go together and which do not, when he begins to listen happily to verses of absurdity."[6] And as soon as a child has learned how something is supposed to be, then it becomes a source of fun to distort it or exaggerate it in some way. The most productive process for making nonsense at the word level among our pairs was the creation of meaningless common nouns and of proper names that are odd or far-fetched.

Assignment of funny names to self, to partner, or to imaginary others reflects awareness of the importance of the normal name and address system. In nonplay exchanges, children are very insistent that they be called by their correct names. Several of them engaged in serious discussions on the choice or the correct pronunciation of their proper names. One girl objected to being called Karen and repeatedly pointed out that her mother called her *Kiren*.

There may be certain properties that make some types of play names especially amusing. Nonsense syllables, like *dingba*, *poopaw*; nonname words, like *Mrs. Fool-Around*; terms with scatological overtones, like *Uncle Poop*; and terms that are potentially insulting but that may also be used of self, like *Silly-face* or *Dumbhead*, served as themes for social play among all groups except the youngest. The following example represents at least two types:

Girl (5:7)	*Girl (5:1)*

(both children are using telephones to call friends)
(1) Mommy, mommy, I got
    new friends called Dool,
    Sol, Ta.

                                (2) Dool, Sue, and ⌒Ta?

           (both laugh)
(3) Those are funny names,
    aren't they?

                                (4) No, it's Poopoo, Daigi,
                                      and Dia . . . Diarrhea.

           (both laugh)

The manipulation of sense and nonsense is one of the components of many successful rhymes and stories written by adults for children, but children also create nonsense. They use outrageous names, juxtapose improbable elements, invent unlikely events, retaining just enough sense of the real world to hold the fabrication together. In several cases the nonsense is produced as if it were serious sense and *marked as play only by laughter after the performance.* With gestures and dramatic delivery, and a straight face, one boy (3:5) told another a story about his Thanksgiving turkey, which was caught, patched up with a bandaid, and cooked. It thereupon flew out the window. Both giggled happily after the narrative.

A girl pretended to write a letter with real paper and pencil. She produced the following poetic nonsense—which must have been her own unique creation and which was heartily appreciated by her partner:

Girl (4:9)	*Girl (4:7)*

(on the car, writing letter)   (listening and drumming on stove)
(1) Dear Uncle Poop, I would
    like you to give me a
    roasted meatball, some
    chicken pox . . .
(2) and some tools. Signed . . .
(3) Mrs. Fingernail. (smiles
    and looks up at partner)

(*continued*)

(4) Toop poop. (laughs)
Hey, are you Mrs. Finger-
nail?

(5) Yes, I'm Mrs. Fingernail.
(in grand, dignified voice)

(6) Poop, Mrs. Fingernail.
(giggles)

Manipulation of sense is often, except in intent, closely related to outright prevarication, and we must presume that when a child misnames or asserts an obvious untruth and marks it as playful, that he has some awareness of the distinction between truth and falsehood. But several factors are involved here, factors having to do with conversational usage.

Play with conversation. Conversation is built on a number of conventions that are actually guidelines for social transactions. Conversing is a highly cooperative venture, even when the tone is truculent or contentious. Linguists, sociologists, and philosophers have only relatively recently begun to study the assumptions about procedures, mutual expectations about content and sequence, and rules for regulating or engineering exchanges that speakers bring to particular speech situations. As a child learns to converse, he acquires these assumptions, expectations, and procedural rules—though even as an adult he may never be able to explicate them in a general fashion. Furthermore, the child learns most of what he knows about the rules for conversing not from explicit instruction but through first-hand experience of interacting with others in a variety of situations. Some "higher-level" guidelines may be verbalized by adults: *You must always tell the truth* or *When I ask you a question, answer me*—but such admonitions are generally addressed to children who already know quite well that truth is expected and that questions require replies.

To return to the topic of "truth," it is important to note that false assertions not only represent mismatches between words and certain events, but they also violate assumptions and expectations that make social interactions possible. One vital rule on which society depends is *Say what you believe to be true* (and not less and not more) or in more familiar words—*the truth, the whole truth, and nothing but the truth.* Play with false assertions is possible only if this social convention is well understood.

Anne Davison at the University of British Columbia has observed the beginnings of play with this discourse convention in two siblings, Sophie (3:2) and Jean (2:0).[7] A still younger child (1:10) did not apparently recognize what Davison calls nonserious speech, but Sophie found misnaming things and pictures in books quite funny—if the interlocutor was her mother. With an unfamiliar adult, however, she was less sure of the humorous intent and was uncertain how to respond. Jean also succeeded in playing with the convention with his mother, though he was easily recalled to seriousness if his mother did not go along with the joke.

Our agemates often broke this truth or sincerity rule with the apparent intent of creating a joke. A boy (5:2) asked a girl (5:5) whom she would rather be with—Mary Ann or Lisa. She looked at him quite soberly and replied *Um. I think . . . um . . . Lisa, because she's a boy.* The she giggled and her partner laughed and said *No, she's a gi::rl. You silly.* Asserting what is not, was not, or probably will not be can serve as a basis for social play only if both partners are aware that the orientation is playful. If that condition fails, then a false statement will be interpreted as deceit or error, not as play.

Children do play with conversational conventions even before they are able to conduct what adults would consider a coherent and "sensible" dialogue. However, the conventions that children can use in a nonplay manner they can also put to playful use. One convention that is quite productive of play can be stated roughly as: If an assertion has been made, and if you must contradict it, provide some support or justification for your contradiction or apologize for countering the assertion. Further, if the person who makes the assertion must reassert his position after being countered, he too must add some support. An example of the near-normal and nonplay use of this convention is:

Girl (2:10)	Boy (3:0)
(they hear a noise outside the room)	
(1) It might be your mommy.	
	(2) No. She's not coming.
(3) She's coming.	
	(4) No, she's not going down to pick me up. Joan is.

The same couple produced a playful episode based on violation of the same convention (as did almost all pairs):

Girl (2:10)	Boy (3:0)
(1) That's your cowboy hat when you go outside.	
	(2) No, no it's not.
(3) I bet it is.	
	(4) No it's not.
(5) Yes it is.	
	(6) No it's not.
(7) Yes it is.	
	(8) No.

A second convention that is both productive and popular for playful distortion is one that builds on what has been called an invitation question. The convention, however, is probably not restricted to questions. In adult conversation it operates somewhat as follows: Respond to a question or assertion concerning your own state or experience as an invitation to contribute to the conversation. Thus, if a conversational partner says to you *I heard that you had an unusual vacation*, a simple *yes* or *no* does not suffice to maintain interaction. As addressee, you have been invited to expand on the topic, for instance, *Yes, we spent a week in Portugal.* Some such convention appears to underlie our agemates' play episodes in which one partner repeatedly questions and the other answers but steadfastly refuses to elaborate. The absence of elaboration is particularly noticeable following a negative response:

Girl (3:7)	Boy (3:7)
	(has just put on fireman's hat)
(1) Is that your fire hat?	
	(2) Yeah.
(3) Did you get it from school?	
	(4) Nope.
(5) From here?	
	(6) Nope.

(7) Where? In the car?

(8) Um, no.

(9) From you?

(10) No.

(11) From in the . . . the
other room?

(12) No. Yes.

A nonplay or literal use of the same convention is, as might be predicted, also possible for this same pair: A: *You changed your mind?* B: *Yes, I want to be the daddy.*

When people talk to each other, they not only convey facts or reveal emotions; they perform meaningful social acts. They warn, promise, command, ask permission. These essential, interpersonal events have been called speech acts. The English philosopher John Austin pointed out that certain formulations do not refer to social acts but are in fact themselves social acts— for instance, an apology is accomplished by saying *I apologize*; one enters into the contract we term "promising" by saying *I promise.* [8] Underlying the successful performance and interpretation of such acts are the shared understandings of the speakers. A successful request for information (a question) rests on the beliefs that the speaker does not already know the answer, that he wishes to know the answer, and that he believes the addressee is able and willing to divulge the answer but is not going to do so without the impetus of the request. Our pairs played with requests for information most often by violating the underlying belief conditions that the speaker did not already know the answer and that he wanted the requested information. In the following example, the pair enjoyed a series of pointless questions and obvious answers:

Boy (5:2)

(picks up dress-up items)
(1) What is this?

(3) What is this?

Girl (5:7)

(sits on car)

(2) It's a party hat.

(4) Hat.

(continued)

(5) Funny. And what is
this?

(6) Dress.

(7) Yuck.
(8) And what is this?

(9) Tie.

(10) All yucky stuff.

Speech, of course, enters into the other aspects of play as a marker of playful orientation, as a means of managing the complex activities of make-believe, and as a component in the expressive behavior of pretending. As we shall see later, much ritualized play is also built on the resources provided by language and speech.

From the vocalizations built on syllable structures to the relatively sophisticated violations of the structure of speech acts or of conversational conventions, almost every type of systematic regularity of language form and use is available for play. The more we understand of the various facets of language use, the better we will be able to identify instances of children's play with the resources of language and communication.

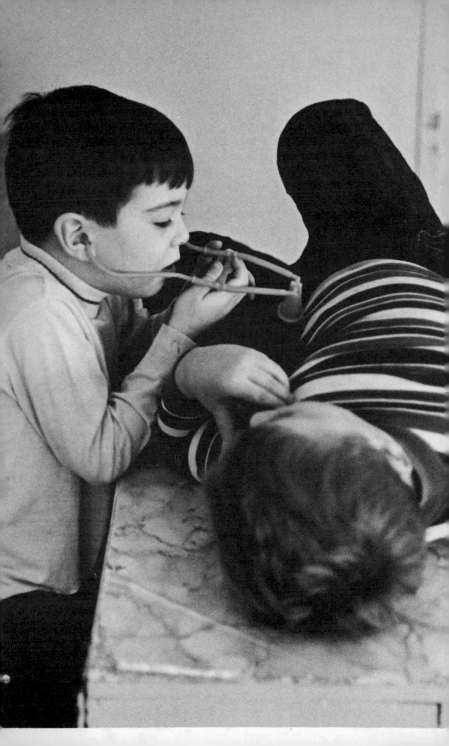

6 / Play with Social Materials

In all the aspects of play, four developmental trends are evident. First there are, obviously, processes of biological maturation, of increasing skill and competence with respect to the varied facets of experience. Second, each aspect of play, as it evolves, becomes more elaborate and tends to combine into more complex events in which two or more resources are used simultaneously —as in rope jumping, which usually combines play with motion and play with language. Third, as play develops, its forms become less determined by properties of the materials in the immediate situation and come increasingly under the control of plans or ideas. This last trend was clearly illustrated in my account of the development of object play. Fourth, as a child's world expands to include more people, situations, and activities, these new experiences tend to be incorporated in his play. In analyzing play with language, we have already begun to see how newly acquired rules for conversation are turned to playful uses.

In this chapter we will examine an aspect of play that reflects the child's rapidly developing competence as a member of his society. Features of the social world, and of socially learned and transmitted expectations of the way objects, actions, and people are related, provide the principal resource of make-believe or pretending. This type of play, when it involves recognizable "characters" and plots of story lines, has also been called dramatic or thematic play. It is perhaps one of the most complex kinds of play conducted in childhood, since it is likely to encompass most if not all of the resources at a child's command and to integrate them into a whole. The principle of integration is some notion or idea, often one that can be named by the child, such as "playing house" or "cops and robbers." There are primarily two kinds of social constructs—socially shared views of the way life is—that serve to integrate pretend play. One is an action plan, a sort of blueprint for arranging actions and events into a coherent episode. The other is the role or identity assumed by the pretender. Roles and plans are intricately interrelated, but it is useful to distinguish them as different kinds of social construct. Indeed, some pretending exhibits a coherent plan without discernible social roles, whereas other pretending appears to rest on adoption of roles with little use of a story line.

It is unlikely that much well-formed pretend play appears before the age of three, and it is generally thought to diminish before adolescence. In an article on the resemblances between imaginative play and private fantasy, Eric Klinger pointed out that "fantasy seems to become frequent after the demise of play."[1] Two somewhat related views have been advanced about the fate of pretending. On the one hand, when overt make-believe play decreases, it may be that make-believing continues but goes underground to become private fantasy or daydreaming. There it is adapted to the characteristic preoccupations of adolescence: popularity, romance, choice of vocation, and achievement of life goals. But at the same time that overt pretend activities decrease in frequency, a different kind of play begins to appear, one that reflects the increasing adaptation of the young person to his social world. Piaget saw the onset of games with rules (especially competitive team games) and the change toward highly realistic symbolic play (such as the construction of elaborately detailed dramas, or inventions of realistic but imaginary countries or epochs) as natural replacements for make-believe.

We will return to questions of the occurrence and functions of pretending at the end of this chapter. But first we must consider the resources available to the child and how they are employed in the service of make-believe.

The linguist Michael Halliday has called the child "one who is learning how to mean."[2] Videotaped records of interactions between parents and children have provided a glimpse of the origins of learning how to mean. The infant's first gestures, whether or not truly responsive and voluntary, are often greeted by the caregiver as if they were intentional. An extension of an arm may be seen as a "reach," and the hand will be grasped; an involuntary grimace may be interpreted as an expression of recognition or pleasure, and the parent will smile back and speak. Similarly, a babbled utterance may be heard as "Mama," and will be immediately repeated or imitated by the mother with considerable pleasure and enthusiasm. The infant may therefore begin to learn how to mean, in the sense of intending or performing purposeful and repeatable acts, by having intention attributed to him. The size of the task that lies ahead of him is immense and hardly conceivable, for so much of what we know and do as human beings in a social world is taken for granted. We are, as Gustav Ichheiser has put it, "blind to the obvious."[3]

Looking at a child's story will strikingly illustrate the features of experience that we tacitly assume we share with others—features of personal relationships, of time, of reference and cause and effect, which a child must presumably acquire as he becomes an accredited human being. The sociologist Harvey Sacks examined the first two sentences offered by a girl (2:9) in response to an invitation to tell a story.[4] *The baby cried. The mommy picked it up.* Built into our interpretation or understanding of these sentences is knowledge of the following obvious but implicit facts. We "know" or surmise that the mommy is the mommy of the baby who cried and that these two individuals belong to or comprise part of a unit we call a family. We know also that the events reported occurred in the same order as the sentences that reported them. Further, we take the first event to be a cause of the second event, and we also feel that the actions described were appropriate and normal. And we can recognize the first utterance as a proper opening for a story, since the initiating event is a problem, a situation that must be resolved or corrected. In some way, the young storyteller was also guided by this same tacit knowledge that allows us to interpret the sentences. Such knowledge is reflected not only in the stories children tell but also, and often in more detail, in their make-believe play.

The social constructs that comprise the resources for make-believe are the child's growing knowledge of classes of individuals and their relationships, of categories and types of goals, and of the possible actions and sequences of action that can be employed to accomplish these goals. To these must be added the "correct" relationship of objects and actions, the expected emotions or attitudes of individuals toward events of various types, and the characteristic combinations of persons and their activities with particular settings and times. The more sophisticated levels of play with objects that develop in the second and third years of life reflect the beginnings of the acquisition and integration of such constructs. Full-scale make-believe presents a still richer and more complex picture of the child's construction of his social world, just at the point when he is learning to take for granted the various aspects of the way this world works.

How, if you were three or four years old, would you go about creating a make-believe play episode with a friend? What kind of knowledge would you have to share? How much of the plan must you make explicit? Are there any ground rules that must be agreed upon? How do you determine the content and the conduct of your pretending?

Adults who may have accidentally or intentionally found themselves engaged in pretending with a child will have noticed that make-believing is not entirely free; one cannot behave *ad libitum.* There are restrictions and, apparently, guidelines for behavior, since a "wrong" move will often be pointed out by the child. One might unknowingly sit down on an imaginary playmate, pour invisible coffee rather than the chocolate syrup on imaginary ice cream, or even forget some essential item of clothing and be told, for example, that *Mommies wear hats.* The Russian psychologist Lev Vygotsky was perhaps the first to emphasize the existence of rules of internal consistency in pretend play and to suggest that spontaneous make-believe often selected and highlighted those features of the world that were most salient to the child at a given time.[5]

WHAT IS MAKE-BELIEVE?

Pretending will be defined here as a voluntary transformation of the Here and Now, the You and Me, and the This or That, along with any potential for action that these components of a situation may have. For such a definition to be workable, one must be able to see when a transformation has taken place, and that is generally achieved by contrasting the transformed with the pre- or post-transformed state. For example, how do we know that a child has adopted the role of wicked witch or working woman? She is most likely to announce her new identity to the playmate, but further she is likely to signal the transformation by speaking in a modified voice, by performing some identifying action, or by moving or gesturing in a manner that contrasts with her normal behavior. Pretending tends to be redundantly marked, and the signals are especially clear at points of transition to and from the pretend state.

One must also be able to tell whether the pretending children can and do distinguish between a situation as it actually is and as they have transformed it. Here, again, the indications are generally explicit. Often, in fact, children discuss features of their immediate or anticipated situation: A: *Is that your firehat?* B: *It's not mine to take home;* or A: *Is this a toy?* B: *No, don't play with it. You might break it.* Reference is also often made to being in or out of a pretend state: *I'm not the dragon anymore. Please don't push me 'cause I'm not the dragon anymore.* We know very little about the criteria children use to distinguish between pretend and what they call "real" or "for real" features of a situation, but there is strong evidence that they believe this to be an important distinction and attempt to apply it appropriately.*

The following example illustrates some of the components of pretending. At the beginning of the excerpt, the girl is holding a baby doll and the boy is watching her put it to bed. At utterance (3) she herself becomes the baby and speaks in a higher-than-normal pitch with whining. The daggers indicate her out-of-baby-role directions to the boy, whose parental role she is prompting. These utterances are produced in her normal speaking voice. At utterance (26) she resumes her own identity and asks a literal question, thus ending the make-believe episode.

Girl (3:3)	Boy (2:9)
†(1) Say, 'Go to sleep now.'	
	(2) Go sleep now.
(3) Why? (whining)	
	(4) Baby . . .
(5) Why?	
	(continued)

*The child's accuracy in making this judgment on any given occasion, or the degree to which his judgment coincides with that of an adult, is another question. Here I only wish to note that all the participants in the pair sessions could make the distinction "real-pretend" and that its application to their interactions was a matter of immediate concern to them.

†(7) No, say 'Because.'
(emphatically)

(6) Because.

(8) Because!
(emphatically)

(9) Why? Because why?

(10) Not good. You bad.

(11) Why?

(12) 'Cause you spill your milk.

†(13) No, 'cause I bit
somebody.

(14) Yes, you did.

†(15) Say, 'Go to sleep. Put
your head down.'
(sternly)

(16) Put your head down.
(sternly)

(17) No.

(18) Yes.

(19) No.

(20) Yes. Okay, I will spank
you. Bad boy. (spanks her)

†(21) My head's up.
(giggles)
(22) I want my teddy bear.
(petulant voice)

(23) No, your teddy bear go
away. (sternly)

(24) Why?

(25) 'Cause he does. (walks off
with teddy bear)

(26) Are you going to pack
your teddy bear?

This exchange illustrates transformations of identity; the girl acting as Parent becomes Baby and finally resumes her nontransformed identity; the boy becomes Parent. These assumed roles import both actions and attitudes which are represented as characteristic and appropriate to the roles. Baby has been naughty, must be scolded and punished. It won't go to sleep, and its toy must be taken away. Baby whines, the Parent speaks sternly. The most striking aspects of the episode, however, are the extent of engineering provided by the girl and her alternating performance as Baby and as director of the scenario. It appears that, even at the age of three, a child can achieve "role distance," at least with familiar roles such as Parent and Baby.

Another example will illustrate a different kind of make-believe, one that does not depend on transformation of identity. It rests on the creation of a telephone call to which is added a virtuoso enactment of a problem situation. The problem is one of sickness; the solution is care and treatment. The performance is a solitary one by a boy whose companion only subsequently acknowledged the situation the boy had dramatized.

Girl (4:9)	Boy (4:9)
	(1) Hey, I have to call my friend Casper. (picks up phone and dials)
	(2) 'Cause he knows Superman's watching him today. (lets phone ring)
	(3) Hello, Casper. How are you doing? (pause)
	(4) What? (gasps)
	(5) Teddy bear got sick? (expression of shock)
	(6) He did? Oh boy! (considerable feeling)
	(7) You know where everything is, right? (slight pause)
	(8) You know where the aspirin is? (slight pause)
	(9) Is he in bed? (pause; (7), (8) and (9) said with more business-like concern)
	(10) Yeah . . . Goodbye, Casper. (hangs up phone and after turning to girl, says seriously)
	(11) I got some bad news to tell you, Kathy.
(12) What?	
	(13) My teddy bear's sick.

(continued)

(14) Oh. (more polite
than really
concerned)

                    (15) But there's a good thing—
                           My friend Casper is home.

In this episode the boy spoke with an imaginary friend, Casper, who may have been a TV character or just invented for the occasion. The boy's reproduction of telephone gaze (eyes fixed on wall) and pausing to allow his friend to respond were highly realistic. He developed the theme of sickness of a pet and proposed the appropriate treatment and care to Casper. After hanging up, he used a conventional routine to tell his playmate what had happened. Her response was perfunctory, but adequate. Note that the pretend episode was framed—that is, announced in advance and recapitulated and evaluated at the end.

From these two examples, we can see that pretending children use resources from the following categories: (1) roles or identities, which are assigned not only to the immediate participants but also to imagined others; (2) plans for action or story lines, which are often combined to form extended dramas; and (3) objects and settings, which are changed or invented as needed. Carrying out the make-believe is largely a matter of communication.

In order to pretend with a companion, the child needs techniques for indicating who he is, what he is doing, what objects represent (or what objects have been invented), and where he is (at home, at work, on a train). Signals of a play orientation, such as giggling or grinning, are of course available, but not always present in pretend play. Explicit directions to a partner are employed as in the first example, and normative statements are often made, such as *Daddies don't carry pocketbooks* or *Little boys don't drink coffee*. Further, the pretend transformations are mentioned, as in the framing of the second example. In our sessions a great deal of talk was devoted to explicit mention of plans, roles, and objects or settings. Questions, descriptions, and suggestions concerning the various components of pretending are illustrated below:

Component		Example
Role:	self	I'm a work lady at work.
	partner	Are you going to be a bride?
	both	We can both be wives.
Plan:	self	I gotta drive to the shopping center.
	partner	Pretend you hated baby fish.
	both	We have to eat. Our dinner's ready.
Object:	change	This is a train. (putting suitcase on the sofa)
	invent	Now this is cheesecake and this is ice cream. (pointing to empty places on a plate)
Settings		Here we are at the doctor's office. This is our house.

In addition to talk about procedures and explicit mention of transformations, another technique for communicating make-believe is enactment. This includes any overt representation by means of content or manner of speech, or content and manner of actions, put forth by the pretender as characteristic of an adopted identity or appropriate for the adopted plan. Pretending to be Baby is enacted by speaking as a baby speaks, saying and doing things a baby would do, reacting to Mommy or Daddy as a baby would, using objects in baby fashion, and expressing babylike needs, desires, and attitudes. Some features of enactment are highly stereotyped; for instance, babies do not (cannot) say "Goo-Goo." Other features of enactment, however, are amazingly realistic. A Mommy, speaking to Baby, shortens and simplifies her utterances; uses terms of endearment; speaks of herself and often uses third-person pronouns for Self and Baby: *That's Baby's food and this is Mommy's food.* She also repeats what she has just said: *Mommy's angry. Yes, Mommy's very, very angry,* and reformulates questions and answers them herself: *Are you tired, Baby? You're tired, aren't you, Baby? Of course you are.* These same characteristics have been widely observed in the speech of adults to very young children.

Some enactments are schematic, representing only salient events in a sequence of actions and omitting details: driving to a store, getting out of a car, getting back in with a milk carton, and returning home—without having parked the car or purchased the milk. Most enactments are clearly created from concepts of appropriate behavior and are most likely not direct imitations of models. For example, a boy who walks into the house announces *Okay, I'm all through with work, honey. I brought home a thousand dollars*, and hands over the money to his beaming Wife has probably not witnessed this scene in his own home. He has, however, generated certain characteristics typical of husbands.

The actual behavior in enactments has been filtered through the child's understanding of his world. Though some enactments consist of purely conventional symbols used to indicate a pretend identity or action, and as such are interesting from the point of view of children's communication, the majority of enactments represent information gained and organized by the child as he learns more and more about the nature of the social world and about himself as part of it.

What are the roles and plans that children have at their disposal? These must differ to some extent across cultures, since they are built on the materials of immediate experience. The major components of pretending were represented among the children we observed, and it is possible to discern some consistent patterns.

IDENTITIES AND ROLES

A pretend space may be populated with various toy animals, people, and imaginary beings. Children can take on the identities of many of these, or can relate to them or talk about them as individuals. The question of animation deserves brief comment, however, before we discuss these role types.

The presence of several large stuffed animals (snake, bear, fish, and a smaller tiger) in the room in our agemate study naturally led to their being animated. Most pairs made the fish swim and the snake wiggle. But more complex than the indication that the snake might slither or bite are those cases in which a child assumed the identity of the animal by speaking for it: *Hello, I'm a baby fish* (said in a high squeaky voice while making the fish swim toward the partner). In another type of transformation the animal was clearly attributed a family role such as Child or Pet, who might also speak or misbehave or require punishment. The stuffed animals could also occupy "functional" roles.

Functional roles are defined in terms of action plans. They are the animate but not necessarily human entities that have specific functions to perform. If, for example, children are engaged in a pretend dinner, both may be diners or one may take the functional role of server. If both are traveling in a car, there must be a driver and a passenger. Functional roles are distinct from family or character roles. A child may simultaneously play a family role such as Mother and the functional role of Cook when preparing a meal.

"Character" roles are of two kinds—stereotyped and fictional. Stereotyped roles are distinguished primarily on the basis of occupation, habitual action, habitual attitude, or personality feature. Examples from our sessions are cowboy, fireman, policeman, Indian chief, bride, wicked witch, doctor, nurse. These types were generally flat in terms of personality, their actions and attributes highly predictable, and their scope of action highly restricted. These characters tended to be associated with appropriate actions, but differed from functional roles in that they could be invoked or adopted without taking part in any action. A boy could say that he wanted to be a fireman or could call a fireman on the phone. A girl could become a bride by putting on a lace curtain, without taking part in a wedding and without having a bridegroom.

Also independent of any specific action was the fictional role. This involved individuals who had proper names and whose source appeared to be stories, television, or oral tradition. Examples are St. George and the Dragon; Santa Claus; Hansel and Gretel; Friedmore Caviters (possibly a TV character, possibly just imagined); Hooey; Cookie Monster; Mr. Donkey; and Dr. Jekyll and Dr. Hines (sic), who were both "good guys." Purely fictive but perhaps only nonce characters were Mrs. Fingernail and Uncle Poop, who had little to offer other than their names, which were considered funny by the children. Few children attempted fictional roles. They were more talked about than enacted. (An exception was a young boy who was either Batman or Robin through the whole session.)

Of great importance were family roles. They usually came in

pairs. One could generally predict, for example, that when a Mommy appeared she would be instantly joined by Daddy or Baby. These roles were treated by the children as if they were always potentially available. They were "there" and needed only to be matched to self or partner or be invoked to be effectively present. These were, of course, Mother, Father, Wife, Husband, Baby, Child (Daughter or Son), Brother, Sister, and much more rarely Grandfather and Grandmother; only one Uncle was mentioned. A Parent, not specifically marked for sex, was sometimes enacted. To be included here is Pet, who was sometimes treated as Child. The stuffed animals were usually drafted for this role.

Family roles can, of course, coincide with functional roles: Mother was usually the server for pretend meals; Father became the defender in the case of danger. Family roles did not coincide with character roles, though they were transformed (reversably) from them. Family roles were stronger than character roles. They were acted out for longer periods of time and, under conditions of transformation, they seemed to be primary; for example, Husband temporarily became a fireman and was then transformed back into Husband.

Transformations occurred across generations but along sex-appropriate lines: Mother → (female) Baby, Daughter → Sister, or Mother → Wife. These roles were always assigned according to the actual sex of each child. A violation of this rule counted as a joke or as an insult and was sometimes used in teasing.

At the fringes of our pretend space, but never on stage, were the peripheral individuals who were discussed or called on the telephone, but whose identity the children never adopted. These were imaginary friends and anonymous guests for whom the house was cleaned and parties planned. Discussions also touched on real but absent people, such as the nursery-school teacher, the third child of the set, or one of the investigators. Their existence was only in the nonplay world, and they did not enter the play space.

Both the sex and the age of the children were factors influencing their choice of which family roles to adopt. As other research findings lead one to expect, boys adopted male roles and girls female roles. This choice was virtually absolute in mixed-sex pairs. In all-male pairs, a few boys adopted some functional role more generally played by girls (like server or shopper) but *never* specified their family role as a female one. In a mixed-sex pair of three-year-olds, a boy who wanted to cook dinner was firmly told by the girl that *Daddies don't cook*. Girls in same-sex pairs were only slightly more versatile, preferring the relational roles of Mother and Child, Wives or Mothers with imaginary children. One girl played doctor to an ailing child, and a good number took on the functional role of repairer (of broken car).

The family role choice was greatly influenced by age. Only Mother, Father, and Baby were enacted by the youngest children, and Mother and Father were also their choices for imaginary telephone partners. Although a few young pairs discussed their "real" siblings and never enacted sibling roles, the older ones talked about Brother and Sister, and occasionally enacted them briefly. They also discussed a few Grandparents and telephoned them several times.

With the increasing age of the pretenders, Baby was replaced by Child, though adult roles were the most favored at all ages. It was not, apparently, much fun to be either Baby or Child. Parents or Husbands and Wives could do more things and could talk more, and Baby or Child was expected to obey and also was liable to be punished or scolded. Two older pairs enacting Mother and Father transformed a stuffed animal to Pet, then to Child. Far more functional and character roles were adopted by the older children as compared to the youngest.

Some functional roles were subject to negotiation, particularly those of driver or passenger in the large wooden car, and driver was preferred. Family roles were often discussed before enactment began. A child assigned the Baby role might declare it was her turn to be Mommy or might bargain for some other role. In one case this was resolved by Mother's inventing an imaginary Baby and her playmate's becoming a nurse. Only among the youngest pairs was a role assignment occasionally rejected outright in favor of the child's own identity. For example, a girl called to a boy *Daddy!* and he replied *I'm not Daddy. I'm Alex.* This response abruptly terminated the interaction. A few minutes later the girl tried again, and again failed to gain a Daddy to complement her own Baby role.

The expansion of the child's world is reflected in these role choices. The youngest children adopted the role that coincided with their actual experience (Baby); or took the *reciprocal* relation to their own experience (Mother or Father). Girls showed much more Mother- or Baby-appropriate behavior than boys, whose Father enactments were less detailed. The older children, however, enacted roles and role pairs that they could not have actually assumed in real life. Not only did they adopt parent roles vis-à-vis an invented or transformed Child, but they represented the relationship, Husband-Wife, or other male-female character roles, and did so in more diverse situations. Husband-Wife roles, however, were drawn in far more detail than were characters (such as the cowboy and the girl; Batman and Cat-Woman).

PLANS

When one child suggests a plan for pretend play, say *We can go on a vacation in a beautiful hotel*, and it is accepted, how do the playmates know what to do next? When a girl shrieks with fear on sighting a stuffed snake, how does the partner know what his actions should be? The majority of the pretend episodes we observed were constructed on a limited number of themes, many of which have been previously reported by other observers in nursery schools. Children seem to have a repertoire of action sequences that can be indicated quite economically and then played out with little discussion of what to do next. I will hypothesize that these themes or action plans are actually constructed by the children, rather than copied or reproduced from some single incident. In enacting relational roles, children obviously select characteristic attributes observed in many different situations and over an extended period. They also "invent" actions or attitudes that may never have been directly experienced but appear to have been inferred from what they know of "real life." Action plans are built up in much the same way.

A plan consists of a sequence of events or actions performed or experienced by a cast of functional roles. The events or actions are associated with characteristic settings and props. A popular plan in the sessions was TREATING-HEALING. The functional roles were patient, healer (who often though not always was identified as doctor), and, optionally, adviser or counselor; the setting was sometimes specified as a doctor's office, sometimes unspecified. The instruments of treatment were transformed or invented props such as a thermometer, medicine, or even food. A school lunchbox in the room served in this plan as a doctor's bag (though in other plans it served as a workman's toolbox or as a lunchbox for Father). The initiating cue that triggered this plan was an announcement of illness, wounds, injury to an animal, or even the death of the Pet. The next step was treatment, which generally led to healing or recovery. The most dramatic announcement was depicted by a girl (5:0) who fell weeping upon her dead Pet (stuffed bear) and cried *He's dead.* Her mother (5:2) solicitously suggested that she give it lots of food and it would come alive again. Despite several attempts, the patient failed to respond to treatment.

The forty-eight acquainted pairs produced fifty-one episodes of a plan we can call AVERTING THREAT. A number of anthropologists and folklorists have also noted the popularity of this theme, even up to age twelve and beyond. The sequence of events for the plan as it developed in our sessions can be divided into three major components:

(1) *Identification of functional roles*
    Source of threat identified (*Here comes a monster*).
    Particular danger noted (*He's going to eat us*).
    Other functional roles (defender and victim) are assigned or enacted. Both children can be victims—both may shriek and flee—or one can be victim and the other defender. Denial of threat is possible (*He won't hurt us*).
(2) *Defense*
    Counteraction by defender (*I'll kill him*).
    Instruments employed (defender may throw dynamite, transformed from toy flashlight).
    Reinforcements can optionally be summoned (*Call our friend the bear to help*).
(3) *Outcome*
    Threat succeeds (*He ate me, I'm dead*).
    Threat is destroyed (*I got him*).
    No clear outcome can be determined.
    A destroyed threat can revive and, if so, the action returns to the first step and recycles again.

An example of an episode built on this plan is taken from a mixed-sex pair. They were at home and in the family roles of Husband (5:0) and Wife (5:2). A fire (source of threat) broke out in the house. The Wife (victim) announced it, and the Husband (defender) extinguished the fire with a hose (stuffed snake, transformed) and provided water noises. The threat then revived as the fire broke out in another part of the house and was again destroyed. It then revived and spread to the sky, whereupon God became the potential victim and the defender (still the boy) had to enlist the help of the "magical" fire snake to destroy the threat. The stuffed animal was transformed again to meet this extraordinary danger.

There were differences in children's performances that related both to age and to sex. Younger pairs were more often both victims, less often defended, and used fewer instruments. Older pairs, even when both members were initially victims, more often introduced a defender. In mixed-sex pairs, it was far more likely that the boy would defend. Only the older children called in reinforcements, and they succeeded in destroying the majority of the threats they faced. In general, these patterns resemble the narrative structures of the stories that children tell.

Other popular plans named by the children which seemed to have the property of unfolding action by action, without extensive discussion of what to do next, were PACKING; TAKING A TRIP; SHOPPING; COOKING; DINING; REPAIRING (anything could be declared broken and then fixed, but the wooden car was most often the object of attention); and TELEPHONING. Each plan had its own inventory of functional roles, and each was carried out alone or combined with other plans to form longer sequences, as when first the car was packed and then the couple drove off on a holiday trip. One basis on which longer sequences are formed appears to involve the interaction of plans and roles.

ROLES, PLANS, OBJECTS

If two children agreed on the assignment of family roles, a number of plans could be joined in a relatively coherent sequence. A pair of three-year-old girls adopted the complementary roles of Mommy (M) and Baby (B). These roles provided a scaffold for several plans and actions. In barest outline these were: M feeds B; M interrupts B's play at stove and warns B to stay away from it; M asks B if she wants to go along to grocery store (when B decides not to go, M drives off alone to buy bread, butter, and milk); a tiny chest of drawers triggers an episode of ironing B's imaginary clothes; B whines and needs to go to bathroom and M takes B to toilet (three-legged stool with glass center); M gives B a toy car (short out-of-role incident as B drives car); M sets table for lunch (out-of-role while M examines toolbelt); B soils her pants; M gives B lunch; M dresses B to take her to Sunday school; B soils her pants again and M prepares to change her. With only a few momentary distractions the two stayed in role for the duration of the fifteen-minute session.

The correct or acceptable selection and execution of plans is a major factor in role enactment. Greater elaboration and more coherent sequencing of plans was observed for familiar roles than for those which the child had not experienced directly (fireman). The relations that hold between roles and action plans require far more systematic study.

Objects in sight also influence the roles that are adopted or assigned. Dress-up clothes certainly suggest further apropriate enactment, and objects appear to trigger the adoption of some plans. Seeing a stove probably increased the likelihood that the children would decide to cook dinner. A miniature toolset often led to the decision that the car needed repair. But the relationship is not always so direct. A pair engaged in AVERTING THREAT succeeded in destroying the monster (snake) by putting him in the oven. The presence of toy telephones in the room probably triggered the large number of telephone calls (eighty-two in all). However, once a plan was embarked upon, object and setting transformations tended to be subject to the requirements of the plan. The observation room or some part of it became a forest, Puerto Rico, a doctor's office, a beach, or a home, as needed.

An enthusiastic and imaginative pretender tends to make do with what is available. A toy flashlight can be tried out as such, but if an instrument is needed to destroy a threat, the flashlight can serve as a pistol or even as a firehose. It is possible to account for many object transformations that might at first seem arbitrary by considering the plan context in which they take place. In carrying out the AVERTING THREAT plan these additional object transformations were made:

(1) Stuffed bear animated as defender.
(2) Stuffed snake animated as source of threat.
(3) Hand became firehose (treated as instrument).
(4) Hand became gun (instrument).

(5) Stuffed snake became firehose (instrument).
(6) Flashlight became dynamite (instrument).
(7) Three-legged stool with magnifying glass became spyglass (auxiliary instrument for spotting fire).

The requirements of the plan or role control the specific transformations that can be made. We have seen that, in the early stages of play with objects, pretending is tied to the perceptual or physical properties of objects. It seems to be the case, however, that once a child reaches a level of cognitive maturity that permits him to operate with roles and plans, he becomes less dependent in his pretending on the real properties of objects. As to the social dimension of pretending, certain props or settings that suggest or permit group activities in which functional roles can be differentiated, such as stores (clerk and customer) or buses (driver and passengers), can encourage social as opposed to solitary play among three or more children.

HOW PRETENDING RELATES TO INDIVIDUAL AND CULTURAL DIFFERENCES

Differences among children in their tendency to engage in imaginative play with roles and plans have been positively related, by means of observation, interviews, and specialized tests, to a number of important cognitive and personality factors. Jerome Singer and his associates have suggested that some children have a stronger predisposition to fantasy than others do.[6] Singer suggests that this "fantasy predisposition" is associated with certain characteristic styles of thinking and feeling. Children rated high on fantasy predisposition tend to enjoy play more, are able to concentrate longer on a single task, and show more self-control while waiting or in submitting to rules. They also produce more numerous and more imaginative ideas. They tend to be divergent thinkers. Divergent production, we have seen, is the generation of novel as opposed to stereotyped responses to problems or situations and is itself characteristic of creative persons. Although a high fantasy predisposition is not directly related to superior intelligence, engaging in make-believe appears to contribute to the flexibility with which a child can approach situations and tasks. Brian Sutton-Smith has suggested that play may heighten the ease with which new approaches or ideas can be adopted toward diverse materials.[7] The imaginative pretender has the experience of manipulating, recombining, and extending associations between words and things, and between things, persons, and actions. Thus it is reasonable to speculate that pretending is one of the experiences that facilitate the development of abstract thought.

Many studies of play in nursery schools in the United States and Europe have reported on the frequencies of pretend play (as opposed to rough-and-tumble or construction activities). Most have also noted girls' preferences for domestic themes and boys' for plans involving transportation or adventure. Researchers have generally agreed that, as children grow and mature, their enactments become more realistic, and their themes or plans are integrated and developed in more complex ways.

There is evidence that a high fantasy predisposition is linked with creativity, that more highly elaborated kinds of imaginative play with roles and plans reflect higher levels of development, and that the content and type of pretend play reflect social experience. The question has been raised whether "sociodramatic" play actually appears in certain cultures or subcultures—a reasonable question, since its free exercise depends on some degree of adult cooperation in providing the time, space, enough privacy, access to props, and, at the minimum, no strong disapproval of make-believing. Thus the home environment probably influences the degree to which children engage in make-believe. Since we also assume that the techniques used in pretending, and the ideas incorporated in it, are products of social learning, the degree to which children create such play may differ along cultural or subcultural lines. The answer is that it does indeed vary across groups.

Anthropologists have reported some cultures in which virtually no make-believe play was observed, but they note make-believe in other non-Western societies, such as the !Kung in the Kalahari. Play themes found in different groups tend to reflect activities important to the particular culture. The children of Hopi Indian settlements, for example, conduct pretend rabbit hunts and play at modeling pottery. Differences in the amount of sociodramatic play among children of different ethnic backgrounds in Israel have been observed in separate studies by

Sarah Smilansky and by Dina Feitelson.[8] They found that young children of Middle Eastern, North Arabic, or Kurdish Jewish immigrants showed comparatively little make-believe. Smilansky argues that its relative absence resulted from family conditions and attitudes and was also associated with a depressed development of cognitive, social, and verbal skills. But on the basis of a large-scale study of the playground and after-school activities of children (aged six to fourteen) in town, village, and kibbutz, from both Jewish and Arabic families, Rivka Eifermann disputed Smilansky's interpretation and claimed rather that make-believe with social themes was not absent, but simply appeared at a somewhat later age in the less advantaged groups.[9]

Separate studies in three eastern cities in the United States have shown that children of lower socioeconomic groups engage in little pretend play, at least in the nursery schools where they were observed. As in the previously cited studies, differences in the children's ages, in observation procedures, and in definitions of the categories of behavior prevent strict comparison among these investigations. Further, one of these studies, by Joan Freyberg, found children with both high and low fantasy predispositions within the lower socioeconomic groups. Freyberg, was able to interview six families of children exhibiting high fantasy and low fantasy characteristics and found very different family profiles for the two types of children. Her results, though based on a small number of cases, suggest that parental support is an important factor in the development of a predisposition to make-believe.[10]

There is, however, another relevant question: Can training, primarily tutoring by an adult, lead children to increase and elaborate this type of play? Here the answer is again a guarded yes. By providing role-playing models, suggesting relations between roles and plans, proposing imaginative situations, and using evocative toys over a period of time (usually at least a month with daily contact), an adult can help children to develop some of the skills needed for make-believe.

The next question, of course, is whether such training and its immediate outcome of more spontaneous pretend play produce significant gains on the tests that measure other important cognitive or social skills. What abilities does training or practice in make-believe promote? The methods of training and modeling that emphasize group activity and the communicative aspects of pretend play have been shown to increase children's cooperative behavior and to contribute to better performance on team problem-solving or construction tasks. Such training also leads to more sensitive role-taking behavior (for instance, selecting appropriate gifts for different members of the family). Modest increments in originality and creativity have been reported after tutoring in imaginative play with toys, dolls, and toy settings. Some increases in verbal skills and language use have also been found after training in sociodramatic play.

Finally, and perhaps most critically, if such gains are shown immediately after training, do they have any lasting effect on the child's subsequent development? There is very little evidence on this question. Freyberg found that, two months after training and testing, the tendency toward increased make-believe play was still evident. Other follow-ups have not been reported.

In conclusion, play with social materials is a reflection of the child's growing notions of his world. Knowledge of the behavior and attitudes appropriate to each sex, though limited of course, has been independently confirmed by other studies of children as young as two and a half. Also there is growing evidence that children of three years of age are aware that others may have attitudes and expectations different from their own. Study of social make-believe shows that the differentiation of self and other, and the behavior appropriate to socially identified persons, classes of objects, and types of goals and plans, are explored and are played with in ways that can be systematically studied.

Roles, plans, and objects are the materials of pretending, and a child can enter the pretend world through any of these means. He can decide to be Daddy and then search for a toolbox and decide to repair the car. Or he can sight a toolbelt and begin to fix the car or imaginary roof, without specifically transforming his identity. Or he can accept the role of Daddy assigned to him by another child, prepare to go off to work, and only then decide that a lunchbox must be taken along. When two or more children pretend together, communication becomes a critical factor in the successful production of make-believe. And in the social conduct of pretending we can see the extent to which children conceive of the family as a system of relationships and as a complex of reciprocal actions and attitudes. Since make-believe enactments and themes reflect the child's notions of his world (though they do not copy them exactly), this aspect of play can provide a rich field for students and observers of social development.

Opposite: !Kung girls dancing the springhare dance (Richard Lee/Anthro-Photo).

7 / Play with Rules

The title of this chapter has two meanings. There is ambiguity in some of the preceding chapter titles as well, but here, specifically, each possible reading refers to a topic that will be discussed below. "Play with rules" can mean that rules accompany or characterize the play. It can also mean that the resource with which the player is engaged is a rule or some sort of limit or constraint. Proponents of Piaget's classification of play into stages have selected the former meaning. According to Piaget, the third and most mature of the stages of play to emerge is "games with rules"—organized, often competitive or team activities, structured by rules that specify the participants and obligate and prohibit moves in the conduct of the play.

I have tried to maintain a distinction between the terms play and game in this book.* The topic has been play, defined as a special subjective orientation to resources. This nonliteral orientation can result in various kinds of playful behavior, many of which resemble activities that can also be carried out in a nonplayful fashion (chasing, preparing supper, arguing). But the play behavior I have described, though it is often orderly, internally consistent, and subject to regulation and procedural corrections by the participant (*Your turn* or *You have to wear a hat*

---

*This semantic problem pervades the literature on play. In French, German, and Russian, one word (*jeu*, *Spiel*, and *igra*) refers at once to both play and game. Translators of the influential works of Jean Piaget and Roger Caillois, for example, must deal with the problem and are sometimes inconsistent in the English words they select. And we ourselves do not, of course, always use "play" and "game" consistently in everyday language to distinguish the different concepts.

or *No, my name is Mr. Caviters, I'm your husband*), lacks certain gamelike characteristics. Games are play activities that have become institutionalized (perhaps in the distant past, perhaps more recently). Childhood games are structured by explicit rules that can be precisely communicated; games can be taught and learned. Their existence depends on acceptance of and adherence to a particular set of rules. Infractions usually carry specific penalties or sanctions. Further, games tend to have traditional names (Drop-the-Handkerchief or Capture-the-Flag), though the names vary across communities and across time. Games have the quality of "social objects"—that is, a game has a clear beginning and end, and its structure can be specified in terms of moves in a fixed sequence with a limited set of procedures for certain contingencies. Thus performances of the same game will be very similar. A particular situated performance can be recalled, talked about, evaluated, or planned in advance. Games, then, are more formal, conventionalized events than are the incidents of spontaneous play. And rules are the essence of games.

This book has not dealt with games, either those that are selected, arranged, and supervised by teachers or parents, or those that are freely chosen and executed by children without adult direction. (Iona and Peter Opie, who studied the games of schoolchildren in Great Britain, have concluded that players overwhelmingly prefer their own games and also that adult-directed games are less favored than those learned directly from other children.[1]) Organized play with games seldom appears (in our culture, at least) until children enter kindergarten or elementary school at five or six. Developmental theory would attribute its appearance at that time to the emerging abilities of the schoolchild to engage in sustained cooperative and competitive social interactions; to plan and to carry out longer and longer sequences of purposive activities; and to exercise self-control and submit voluntarily to restrictions and conventions. These emerging capabilities rest, of course, on the reciprocal interaction of the child's experiences with his physical, cognitive, and emotional growth. Few researchers have studied the beginnings of play with games or have related the games of childhood to the more spontaneous kinds of play described in the preceding chapters.

It is possible that the games with rules of later childhood actually have their roots in the earliest playful experiences of infancy. Perhaps the notion of playing by the rules can be traced to the repetitive and predictable patterns that children learn in their interactions with adults. Jerome Bruner and his associates have studied a number of mother-infant pairs, observing how initial regularities in procedure evolve into rule-structured events.[2] Most of the pairs played Peek-a-Boo. Peek-a-Boo shows clear differentiation of participant roles and an internal structure comprised of moves apportioned between the players. Each repetition of the game rests on the same sequence of moves, though certain variants in the execution of each move are permitted. What makes a good game of Peek-a-Boo is the mutual respect of each participant for the rules—that is, their shared expectations concerning what happens next and their willingness to conform to the agreed-upon procedures.

An outline of the essential structure of the game in its developed form is presented below. This form is usually achieved by the time the child is about a year old.

	Initiator's turn	*Recipient's turn*
Round 1:		
Move 1	Attract R's attention	Give attention to I
Move 2	Hide object, self, or R, optional vocalization	Look for
Move 3	Reveal	Appreciate
Move 4	Reestablish contact	Reestablish contact
	(simultaneous)	
Round 2:		
	Optional repetition of the whole game, with or without permissible variations	

Younger children are usually the recipients, but after the first year many children take the initiator role, hiding self or mother. Permissible variants include vocalizations, changes in who or what is hidden, and what is used to conceal the hidden person or object.

These observations suggest that games with rules have a natural history that begins with the first experiences of the social world. A child needs help from others in learning how to join a game and in discovering the pleasures that can be derived from rule-structured activities. At first, supportive adults provide the controlled variation of timing and movements from which he begins to derive his notion of rule-governed events. The first "team" is usually composed of infant and adult, and cooperation in producing the alternating or simultaneous moves of a game is the basic principle to be learned. Only much later will the child be able to enter into games with less familiar persons, and then only if his playmates also know and respect the rules.

The first successful peer games are likely to be cooperative ones, like Ring-around-the-Rosies. Games based on competition —where one team or person strives to win or to defeat the other —become popular somewhat later, at about seven to nine. Although a younger child is at times contentious and tries to rival a playmate's claims or actions (*I'm stronger than you are*), the demands of organized, competitive play are too much for him. To be forced to give up a turn, to lose an object, to accept the status of loser, are difficult experiences. The child will learn to accept such conditions only when his desire to excel is strengthened and supported by the opinions and reactions of his peers.

That rules themselves can be the resource for play is the second meaning of my chapter title. Violating a convention, upsetting an expectation, or taking apart things that should go together—all can be factors in most of the types of play already discussed. One example of enjoyment in using an object incongruously is provided by a boy of two who delighted himself by trying on a hat, then putting a sand bucket upside down on his head, and finally topping himself with one of his father's large rubber galoshes. In fact, Bruner has aptly described play as "a special way of violating fixity."

There is an aspect of play, however, that takes rules, limits, or constraints as the focal material. Risking the consequences of transgressing the boundaries of the permissible or the possible appears to be the source of pleasure. Such play has been described primarily in its adult manifestations. Roger Caillois included "chance" as one of the basic psychological factors that motivate play and games.[3] Erving Goffman, in an article entitled "Where the Action Is," pointed out the fascination with testing limits, taking chances, and running risks (as, say, in gambling or skydiving).[4] If this attraction becomes obsessive, revocability and freedom are lost, and the orientation ceases to be playful.

How do children play with rules and limits? Some familiar examples will indicate the diversity of constraints that can be challenged by school-age children. Testing the limits of one's abilities is the basis for many games of skill. In playing Statues, children attempt to hold the position in which they have fallen as long as is physically possible. In Follow-the-Leader, there is physical challenge (walking on top of a wall, jumping ditches) and an element of psychological daring as well. Inviting fear, and giving over to it, is pleasurable as long as the child "knows" that the situation is manageable or that he is ultimately in control. Voluntary submission to frightening experiences (sometimes called "thrill seeking") underlies the popularity of ghost stories, roller coasters, and monsters, from the Barong of Bali to our own Frankenstein.

Testing the limits of what another person will tolerate is also common; the danger in this case is precipitating a serious breach of friendship. Consequently, this type of play is often ritualized, so that its nonliteral force is made clear. William Labov has described the ritual insults created by black adolescents in New York.[5] What is said is outrageous and often vicious (*Your old man so poor your family have to paint the furniture on the wall*), but the semantic and syntactic structure of the insults marks them as different from nonplay assaults. These attacks generally follow the formula: addressee's relative (mother, father) is so X that Y, where X is derogatory (old, ugly, dirty) and Y is some unpleasant consequence (*Your mother so old she fart ashes*). The insult must be patently false; if it comes too close to the truth the victim could interpret it as literal and take offense. But a "good" ritual insult is understood as such, and the victim then retaliates in kind.

Among the children in our pair sessions, two major types of limits or constraints were playfully challenged. One type might be called prohibitions by adults—either inferred or invented. We did not tell the children they had to stay in the observation room; on the contrary, the opportunity to explore it was presented as a treat. Nevertheless, several played as if it were forbidden to open the door. Two would take turns opening the door, peeking out, then closing the door abruptly and running to the other side of the room *as if* they did not want to be caught at the "naughty" act. The play was accompanied by whispers and giggles. Similarly, several children noticed the microphone hanging from the parrot's perch and seemed to know that it was adult property rather than a toy. So an inferred prohibition was violated by several boys who stood on the car and pretended to touch the microphone. Some partners thought this was funny; others were somewhat uneasy.

The second type of constraint that was playfully violated involved the relations between the children themselves. Some teasing did occur, mostly of a good-natured variety. But taunting someone is always dangerous. In breaking the rules of interpersonal conduct, the aggressor risks a serious fight. In our sessions, one child would taunt another to a point where we, as observers, felt that the victim was about ready to take offense. Then the aggressor would desist, sometimes spontaneously, sometime in response to a warming issued by the victim in a nonplay tone of voice: *If you do that again, I won't be your friend.* A girl (5:0) teased her male partner (4:9) by repeatedly calling to him, *Goodbye, Mother.* In spite of his protests (*I'm not a girl. You're the Mother*), she persisted, apparently pleased with his distress. At last, almost in tears, he stopped her by saying *I will tell on you.* A boy (5:1) teased a girl (5:2) by "stealing" her pans and cooking utensils one by one and hiding them. For a while she pretended to be angry and retrieved each one, but finally when he announced *I stealed your cake* she terminated the episode by saying *I don't care. It's not a cake anymore.* Among the acquainted pairs, teasing never quite exceeded the tolerable limits. In a few unacquainted pairs, teasing led to real unpleasantness, perhaps accidentally, perhaps intentionally.

Play with rules, in both senses of the term, appears at an early age, becomes increasingly complex, and combines with the other aspects. We can speculate that by playfully violating conventions or testing limits—especially those imposed by the consensus of the peer group—a child not only extends the knowledge of his own capabilities but also learns about the nature of social rule systems. Since societies and personalities are both shaped by rules, a better understanding of the beginnings of such play is essential to the study of human development.

8 / Ritualized Play

One of the most interesting features of spontaneous play is ritualization. Rituals, as I use the term, can be based on any resource: motion, object play, language, social conventions; even play with rules can be performed in a ritualized manner. A ritual, then, is defined not by its content or by the resource it builds on, but by its distinctive form: controlled repetition. The nature of the control is generally rhythmic, and the behavior takes on a predictable regularity of tempo. The scale or intensity (as well as the timing) of a performance may also be controlled, so that both the amplitude and frequency of the actions can be grossly exaggerated or sharply attenuated. For example, in the agemate sessions a particular episode of object play performed by several pairs involved the three-legged stool with the magnifying glass. After it had been discovered and its particular property explored, most children would fetch different objects, place them one by one under the glass, and look at the distorted images, invariably finding the result amusing. But one pair created a ritual out of this experience. One boy placed a hat under the glass and said dramatically *That's the biggest hat I ever saw in my life!* His partner said *Let me see*, looked, smiled, and sat back. Then the first boy put his hand under the glass and said *That's the biggest hand I ever saw in my life!* with exactly the same timing and intonation as before. The partner repeated his request and the same movements, then looked expectantly at the leader, who reproduced his part with a different object but with the identical gestural and verbal rhythms. In this chapter I will describe some of the structural characteristics of ritual play, treating ritualization as a feature that can be added to the various types of play.

An example based on play with a conversational convention (for instance, trying to support a contradictory response or a reaffirmation of a statement) will illustrate the timing features of ritual play. The extreme regularity of each exchange would be far more strikingly displayed by an audio recording, but the timing (in seconds and tenths of seconds) of each utterance and each pause between speakers will indicate the precise regulation of behavior that each child achieved. Throughout this ritual, there was no direct gaze. The boy faced the girl, but she did not look at him.

The content is repetition of a fairly common type of exchange, an assertion and counterassertion or contradiction. Thus the basic resource is play with language. But it is the form and timing that mark this example as a ritual. The pause between speakers is a little longer than might be expected in a normal conversational version of this kind of exchange. Here the pause seems to count as a beat in the rhythm. Throughout the ritual proper (which began after utterance 2) the interspeaker pause varied between 0.5 and 0.7 seconds. The length of each speaker's utterances is also remarkably regular. The girl's and the boy's utterances vary between 0.9 and 0.5 seconds. There also seems to be a relationship between the lengths of the utterances: both speakers first speed up, then both lengthen their utterances in approximately the same way as the ritual progresses. The mood of the ritual is not argumentative; the delivery might be called singsong. There is a progressive rise in pitch throughout and a slight decrease in loudness until the last exchange is almost whispered.

Rituals can be created from almost any kind of content. A nonverbal ritual built on alternating physical gestures was conducted by a boy and girl. They had discovered the net curtains, inspected them, and discussed just what they might be (to make tents? to wear?). Then the boy said *Watch this*, and threw a curtain up over his head. As it floated down, he giggled. The girl then said *Watch this*, and did the same thing. They alternated turns, each beginning with an announcement and ending with giggles, and each attended to the other's turn in the action. There were four pairs of turns. Finally the boy concluded the episode by saying *I'm tired*.

Girl (3:6)	utterance	pause	utterance	Boy (3:7)
(1) . . . no, you're already at the snakes.	—			
		1.2	1.2	(2) No I'm not. (sitting on car)
RITUAL:				
(3) You are too. (ironing)	0.9	0.6		
		0.6	0.9	(4) No I'm not.
(5) You are too.	0.5	0.6		
		0.6	0.5	(6) No I'm not.
(7) You are too.	0.5	0.7		
		0.6	0.5	(8) No I'm not.
(9) You are too.	0.5	0.5		
		0.5	0.5	(10) No I'm not.
(11) Yes, you are too. (wanders across room)	0.5	0.5		
		0.6	0.6	(12) No I'm not.
(13) Yes, you are too.	0.7	0.6		
		0.7	0.7	(14) No I'm not.

(continues through two more exchanges)

This ritual serves to introduce the terms needed for an analysis of more complicated ritual structures. Each person's contribution is called a "turn." This unit of behavior appears to have psychological validity in the sense that, if one person fails to take his turn within the time provided by the rhythm of the ritual, the partner will point out his failure: *You go next* or *Your turn*. In this simple ritual one pair of turns constituted a "round."

> Boy's turn: *Watch this.* (throws curtain, giggles)
> Girl's turn: *Watch this.* (throws curtain, giggles)

The round also appears to have psychological validity as a unit since if a partner suggests *Let's do that again* or *Want to do it again?* a pair of turns (the whole round) is repeated. Features of timing also support the validity of these units.

The content of the curtain ritual is basically motion—throwing curtains up and allowing them to drift back down on top of the head. The phrase *Watch this* marks the focus of action for each turn, and the giggles mark the end of the turns. Since the content of each turn is identical, this type of turn pattern is designated as A-A. The specific content of the turn does not matter; it is classed as A-A if the second child's turn duplicates the content of the first child's. Thus a verbal ritual composed of the identical turns (*Hi, Mommy—Hi, Mommy*) has A-A type content.

A more complicated round can be composed of two turns, where the second turn contains a "paradigmatic" substitution— that is, it substitutes an item from the same class as the first. This sort of relationship would be designated $A-B_p$ (the subscript p denotes a paradigmatic substitution). Examples would be: *Hi, Mommy—Hi, Bubba; —It's blue—It's green*. In the first case, a name was substituted; in the second, an adjective.

But rounds rather than turns are the building blocks of rituals, and the way in which one round follows another must also be distinguished. Thus, a simple ritual starting with an $A-B_p$ round could go on to repeat that round in identical form or could modify it in some way. A ritual composed of three identical rounds (R_i) is:

	Round type	First child	Second child	Turn content type
Round 1	R	Hi, Mommy.	Hi, Bubba.	A-B$_p$
Round 2	R$_i$	Hi, Mommy.	Hi, Bubba.	A-B$_p$
Round 3	R$_i$	Hi, Mommy.	Hi, Bubba.	A-B$_p$

A still more complex relationship may be formed from a possible response to the first turn (for example, *You're a girl.—No I'm not.*) rather than from a substitution of an item from the same class (*I'm a monkey.—I'm a donkey.*). The possible response could be verbal, or it could be some nonverbal gesture that could normally complement or complete the content of the first turn. This type of content relationship, which creates a possible conversational sequence, is called "syntagmatic," and such a turn content is coded A-B$_s$. In the following example, rounds composed of A-B$_s$ type content are repeated identically (R$_i$):

	Round type	First child	Second child	Turn content type
Round 1	R	You're a girl.—No I'm not.		A-B$_s$
Round 2	R$_i$	You're a girl.—No I'm not.		A-B$_s$

Rounds, however, can be modified as they are chained together in an episode. A modified round (R$_m$) built from syntagmatic turn content was created as one child tried to guess the name of his partner's mother:

	Round type	First child	Second child	Turn content type
Round 1	R	It's Linda.	No.	A-B$_s$
Round 2	R$_m$	Adam.	No.	A-B$_s$
Round 3	R$_m$	Crocodile.	No.	A-B$_s$
Round 4	R$_m$	Fish.	No.	A-B$_s$

(continued for seven rounds)

So far only symmetrical turns have been illustrated: one turn per person. Still more complex rounds can be built of nonsymmetrical turns; one person can have two turns to his partner's one. Rounds composed of nonsymmetrical turn structure can also be "done again." The following example of a round has syntagmatic content in each turn and also has asymmetrical turn distribution:

First child	Second child	Turn content type
I'm going to work.	You're already at work.	A-B_s
No I'm not.		C_s

If this round, which is composed of three sequential, syntagmatic turns, were repeated intact, the second round would be coded R_i. But in fact this ritual was still more complex. The second and third rounds were progressively changed. Thus they were coded R_m for modified round:

	Round type	First child	Second child	Turn content type
Round 1	R	I'm going to work.	You're already at work.	A-B_s
		No I'm not.	(pause)	C_s
Round 2	R_m	I'm going to school.	You're already at school.	A-B_s
		No I'm not.	(pause)	C_s
Round 3	R_m	I'm going to the party.	You're already at the party.	A-B_s
		No I'm not.	(pause)	C_s

The modified rounds were related by substitution in an utterance of members of the same class (*to work, to school*). Thus the round modification principle was paradigmatic. (The internal structure of each round, however, was built on syntagmatic turn relations.)

A complete ritual is provided below with coded analysis. A change of turn patterning occurs after the third round, and this change of format was marked by a slight pause and a distinct shift in pitch and volume. The creators of this ritual were a girl (4:4) and a boy (3:9).

	Round type	Amy	Ben	Turn content type
RITUAL:		(1) I can see this.		
			(2) I can't see Amy.	
Round 1	R	(3) I can see Ben.		A-B$_s$
			(4) I can't see Amy.	
Round 2	R$_i$	(5) I can see Ben.		A-B$_s$
			(6) I can't see Amy.	
Round 3	R$_i$	(7) I can see Ben. (slight pause)		A-B$_s$
			(8) Can't see Amy.	
Round 4	R$_m$	(9) Can't see Ben.		A-B$_p$
			(10) Can't see Amy. Trashcan!	

The ritual proper begins with utterance (2), as Ben, seated on the car, picks up on a comment Amy made while looking into the mirror. The first round is composed of utterances (2) and (3) and their intervening pause. Four rounds are completed before Ben concludes the ritual by breaking the format with the exclamation *Trashcan!* As the ritual begins, the interspeaker pauses become very brief. The longer pause between utterances (7) and (8) coincides with a change in round pattern from R$_i$ to R$_m$ and the change in turn content from A-B$_s$ to A-B$_p$. Within each round, the pitch and stress patterns for each speaker were virtually identical, although the number of syllables each produced was different. When Ben modified the last round with utterance (8), and with it the final pitch direction, Amy copied this change exactly. Further evidence on the temporal cohesiveness of ritual play as contrasted with normal interaction is the fact that on the average this pair spoke once every four seconds throughout their seventeen-minute session; during the ritual, however, they spoke on the average every two seconds.

Rituals have several other interesting features. They are clearly set off from other activities by their characteristic style of production. Transitions to and from other activity are easily identified. Sometimes the rituals are even "framed"; that is, the children clearly signal to each other when one begins or ends. And a ritual can be interrupted for procedural corrections. One child can tell the other what to do, momentarily breaking the rhythm and formal structure. Then the ritual is resumed as if no break had taken place. Sometimes one child asks the other what to do next or requests some information he needs to execute his turn. The following example illustrates both framing and embedded procedural clarification. A girl and a boy were carrying on a desultory conversation as the girl packed the suitcase and the boy inspected and handled the several stuffed animals. He showed the fish to the girl and asked in normal conversational voice *Can you carry this?* She replied in a normal voice. Next he gave the fish to her and said *You can't even carry it.* Then the ritual began. Its nonverbal components are indicated in parentheses; the framing material and the embedded clarification sequence are italicized. The ritual begins with the second clause of utterance (3).

Boy (5:2)	Girl (5:7)
(1) *Can you carry this?*	
	(2) *Yeah, if I weighed 50 pounds.*
(3) *You can't even carry it.*	

RITUAL

Can you carry it by the
string?

(4) Yeah. Yes I can.
(lifts fish overhead by
string)

(5) Can you carry it by the
eye?

(carries it by eye)

(6) Can you carry it by the
nose?

(7) *Where's the nose?*

(8) *That yellow one.*

(9) *This?*
(carries it by nose)

RITUAL

(10) Can you carry it by its
tail?

(11) Yeah.
(carries it by tail)

(12) Can you carry it by its
fur?

(carries it by fur)

(13) Can you carry it by its
body?

(carries it by body)

(14) Can you carry it like this?
(shows how to carry it by
fin)

(carries it by fin)

(15) *I weigh 50 pounds almost,
right?*

(16) *Right.*

This ritual combined both language and motion. The boy's
turns were verbal, the girl's primarily variations of picking up
and carrying the fish. The turn pattern of the seven-round ritual
was A-B$_s$: it was syntagmatic because the girl's actions were
normal responses to the boy's indirect requests for action. The
rounds were symmetrical. Each round was modified (R_m), and
the nature of the round modification was paradigmatic. The successive changes in each round were formed by substitution in the
initiating turn, *Can you carry it by X?* where X is successively
string, eye, nose, and so on. Utterances (7) to (9) interrupted
the ritual for a brief check on fact, but the ritual resumed imme-

diately. Utterance (10) had the same intonation as utterance (6). All of the boy's ritual phrases had the same intonation pattern.

Two important trends in the form of rituals across age groups were noted. First, there was a tendency for the older pairs to create the more complex rituals, that is, those with three-turn rounds (asymmetrical rounds) and those with modified rounds. The second trend was the preference of the younger pairs for longer rituals. With minor procedural interruptions and minor format changes, the *Hi Mommy—Hi, Bubba* ritual continued for two minutes.

Repetition and repetition-with-variation have long been recognized as characteristics of early play. They are characteristic also of certain kinds of adult behavior. They constitute a formative principle in magical incantations and spells, religious chants, cheers for football teams, political rallies, riots, in fact many events where members of a group must be synchronized to express solidarity. For children, repetition is apparently enjoyable for its own sake, even in solitude, but in an intimate social situation it provides a basis and framework for continued interaction. In terms of the content, such interaction is relatively inexpensive: no new topics, ideas, or opinions are required. In the rituals each child controls very precisely the behavior of the other, and this regulation is itself satisfying—a form of mastery play, where what is mastered is the control of one's own and one's partner's actions. But these explanations are only speculation—we do not know why children engage in rituals, but we know that they do so and to some extent how they do it.

The study in which pairs of unacquainted children were observed in the same playroom produced rituals also, though somewhat fewer on the average. This kind of social interaction, then, is presumably not unusual, but is probably only rarely produced in nursery schools. Its breeding ground is relatively quiet, undistracted togetherness. What is surprising about the rituals is the extent to which the participants are able to establish and maintain the patterns of exchange, the alternating turns, the sequencing of rounds, and the precise timing. The synchronization of utterance and pause durations indicates a far greater ability to attend to and to adapt to a partner's behavior than has generally been attributed to preschool children.

A ritual is unmistakably play. It exhibits all the descriptive characteristics by which instances of play are recognized. It is apparently enjoyable, performed for its own sake rather than for a goal such as information exchange or the resolution of a disagreement. It is quite spontaneous and engages both partners in precision performances. Rituals are generally based on some other behavior that *could be performed* as nonplay, like peeking out of the door, exchanging greetings, asking and answering questions, and so on. Finally, rituals are very clearly marked as nonliteral by their repetition and by their highly controlled rhythmic execution.

The message, "This is play," is emblazoned on the ritual.

9/ Learning to Play

In the healthy young of most mammalian species, play seems to arise quite spontaneously. In some species, it also appears to survive through the period of dependency with little help or attention from the parent; in others, adults may have some influence on the course of play development through modeling or direct participation in play activities. It has been observed, for example, that some anthropoid mothers attract and even encourage appropriate play partners for their infants. The play of most young animals, however, is either solitary or limited to littermates or other juvenile members of the group or herd. In the human species, parents generally provide the principal environment and partner for early play experiences. Related to the difference in human and animal play is the variety and complexity of the learning tasks that must be accomplished during human childhood. In this prolonged period of dependency and immaturity, children acquire a number of diverse skills and lay the foundations for further learning. The diversity of types of play and the resources used for play parallel the demands and opportunities that human societies will present to the developing child. In this chapter we will ask how and in what ways the child learns to play. We will also examine in some detail what a child who engages frequently and successfully in social pretend play must have already learned.

Simple play with motion and with objects seems to emerge without prompting in the healthy infant. Even earlier, the infant has discovered the pleasure in little bouts of face-to-face interaction with a playfully responsive caregiver. When the infant realizes that a glance or smile can inspire the caregiver to make captivating noises and funny faces, it displays all the signs of intense delight—and repeats the cues that elicit those amusing displays. But soon after, new ways of playing appear. The play routines that caregivers construct with young toddlers are to some extent idiosyncratic to each family. Perhaps each toddler develops some kind of teasing game with a parent that involves first getting the adult's attention and then performing some sort of "forbidden" act. This is followed by the adult's exaggerated protest and the child's laughter and retreat or abstention from the act, after which they immediately repeat the complete routine. The specific content of the routine, however, can be very different across families (for example, the forbidden act may be touching a knob on the TV or starting to open a drawer) as are the specific vocal or gestural signals used by each partner to mark successive moves in the game. The routine and its component signals become increasingly conventionalized as each partner learns the game's design. The child's first experiences with play will take place in the context of its principal social relationships, and the play itself will influence the nature of these changing relationships.

PLAY WITH PARENTS

Infants and young toddlers quickly learn to turn to different people for different kinds of play. Even a very young infant has probably experienced more touching and movement in playing with its father than with its mother. In many families, the very young child finds that the father is often a more exciting playmate, who engages in bouncing or chasing and nice, loud noises. The mother is a better choice for quieter toy play and will likely provide more suggestions for what to do with various toys while not interfering with interesting new ideas. In general, she will also talk more and follow details more carefully, although she may provide more specific guidance if the child is a girl than if it is a boy. The child is not, of course, actually aware of the fact that the mother's play is rather more didactic than the father's and that she also has an agenda for what the child should learn (as well as just enjoy) in the course of certain activities. Nor is the child aware that the kinds of toys usually made available are those its parents consider appropriate to its sex or that the father, in particular, does not encourage the child, if it is a boy, to play with toys considered more suitable for girls. Indeed, parents' indication of their approval of various types of toys may be quite subtle—a smile or an enthusiastic gesture when they offer the child a sex-appropriate toy or longer involvement in play during the child's engagement with a particular object. Nonetheless, the child learns a great deal about sex-appropriate toys during its first two years of life. And as the child becomes more certain of its own gender, it also develops a real preference for those toys and the kinds of activities they permit. Children, whether boys or girls, may come to expect that when they bring a certain kind of toy to the parent, certain consonant activities are likely to follow. For example, a set of dishes will probably initiate a pretend tea party and quiet, intimate talk; a puzzle may lead to a discussion of shapes and colors; and a truck can involve a cooperative father in crawling around on the floor while making appropriate vehicle noises.[1]

In respect to symbolic play, it was previously thought that such play was initially solitary, that it emerged as a function of the child's maturing cognitive capability for symbolic representation and its exploratory gestures with objects and familiar actions. In research on the development of symbolic play, the young child was often observed for a relatively short time in a laboratory where it was provided with a standard set of toys (often while sitting in a high chair). The mother was requested to refrain from initiating play or engaging in the child's activities. Lack of videotaped records that could reveal brief glances and facial expressions or the investigators' focus on the child's handling of the toys precluded observation of subtle communicative gestures between mother and infant. The instructions to the mother, of course, also precluded observation of pretend actions that were suggested or otherwise initiated by the mother. Recent studies indicate, however, that the emergence of symbolic play in the home environment may be socially supported. Certainly, the child of eighteen or twenty months who is discovering how familiar actions can be interestingly reproduced outside of their normal, utilitarian context and how one can use replica objects for such ends is not quite ready to share symbolic actions with a peer. Caregivers, however, appear to be not only intimately involved in many of the first symbolic play behaviors but also influential in encouraging the growth of early pretend play, just as they are in the early stages of language acquisition. We might suspect that in both realms of representation, the meaningfulness of even fleeting symbolic behavior must be recognized and validated by a caregiver if it is to enter into processes of systematic growth.

Just how mothers may foster the growth of very young children's symbolic play was examined in a laboratory setting by Arietta Slade.[2] She observed the interactions of sixteen mother-toddler pairs twice each month when the children were twenty, twenty-two, twenty-six, and twenty-eight months old, arranging that at each session, the mothers would be occupied in conversation with the experimenter for part of the time and the child would be encouraged to play alone. In the final ten minutes, the mother was left alone with the child, and the pair could play freely with an assortment of toys. The duration and the developmental level of the child's symbolic play were analyzed to determine the effects of the mother's involvement (or lack thereof) across this age span, during which symbolic play increases in both complexity and duration. Mothers' involvement was distinguished as more active when they actually initiated the play or took part in it and as more passive when they only contributed suggestions and comments on the child's own activity. Mothers' commentary alone did have the effect of lengthening the play beyond the duration observed for solitary play, but only for children at twenty-six months. But when the mothers actively joined in, their suggestions and participation, both in initiating and carrying out the activities, helped children at all ages to display developmentally higher levels of play. Children whose mother is available and interested are reassured, but if she provides interpretations of actions and both shows and tells how things go together and what could happen next, they are encouraged to engage in their most mature pretend behavior.

In other research, closer examination of how some mothers model and support symbolic play at home indicates that before the child is eighteen months old, mothers tend to comment primarily on the feelings or possible actions of dolls or toy animals in initiating a play episode.[3] They continue this kind of commentary with slightly older toddlers but make a greater percentage of such symbolic attributions (*Oh, the bunny is scared*). When the children themselves begin to make fantasy statements, the mothers are able to respond to them and to add descriptions of the child's actions. When children reach about twenty-four months, however, mothers use questions as well, both naming the child's actions, or identifying their meaning, and seeking a response (*Is the dolly tired?* as the child puts the doll into bed). Repeating the child's comments in questions is effective in sustaining play, but more probably it is the mothers' proposals of play themes and suggestions of what could happen next that further the development of coherent symbolic play episodes and help children make sense of this intriguing new way of playing. As fascinating as pretend activity may be for the child, having an enthusiastic partner, especially one who offers such appealing ideas and can put words to the actions the child seeks to depict, must promote the growth of pretending. Young children certainly know more than they are able to say, but they also seek confirmation that what they are doing is intelligible as they experiment with how things work and what people do.

In a longitudinal study of nine children, who were videotaped in their homes from their first through fourth birthdays, Wendy Haight looked at the interactions of the children, their mothers, their siblings, and their friends.[4] Using a rigorous and detailed definition of social pretending that excluded exploratory gestures, functional uses of objects, literal naming, and such activities as singing or reciting nursery rhymes, she examined the emergence and growth of pretending. At twelve months, four of the children displayed brief pretend gestures, but by twenty-four months, all of them were pretending, some for as long as twenty minutes in a three- to four-hour observation session. The average duration of an episode was almost one minute. Play at thirty-six and forty-eight months increased dramatically in frequency and in the duration of episodes. Haight also found that although at twenty-four months most of the pretend play occurred during the first hour of observation, for the older children the situation was reversed; more play time and longer episodes of pretending were recorded during the last two hours of the observations. These findings call into question the usual brief interaction sessions of children in laboratories, which may well underestimate the natural incidence of such play.

How much of this early pretending was directed at or shared with another person? For children at twelve months, 75 percent of such play was social; by twenty-four months, 80 percent was social. At these ages, the mother proved to be the playmate for almost 90 percent of the time spent in pretending. She was also the initiator of virtually all the pretend play episodes at twelve months and of more than half of them at twenty-four months. These mothers were clearly vital partners in the early growth of symbolic play, not only modeling play behavior for their children, but also conveying the idea that pretend play is an acceptable, even a desirable type of social activity. By thirty-six months, the mother was still the most frequent partner, although social pretend play with siblings was also common at this age. By forty-eight months social play with siblings and friends increased so that, on average, the mother was the partner only half the time.

Surprisingly, even when the children were forty-eight months of age, mothers still initiated almost half of the pretend interactions. Because most studies of pretend play in the preschool period have been conducted in daycare centers or nursery schools rather than in the home, the continuing role of many mothers in supporting social pretending, even during the period when interactions with peers are becoming quite skilled and complex, has been overlooked. It is probably the case, however, that at this time, pretend play with peers and pretend play with mothers has begun to diverge in function, form, and even content. Mothers often use such play to divert a child from a forbidden or dangerous activity, or they incorporate some sort of "lesson" in the play activity to show how something works, how one should behave, or what may happen at, for example, a birthday party or the doctor's office. But mothers and peers are likely to go about constructing a pretend scenario somewhat differently. They probably also differ in their ideas of what constitutes an exciting or amusing plot. Detailed comparison of spontaneous peer-child and caregiver-child play interactions would be a necessary and interesting next step in learning how different relationships and different partner capabilities affect the way children go about pretending.

PLAY WITH SIBLINGS

A sibling is more a peer than a parent, but perhaps less a peer than a friend or a nursery school classmate. If siblings are relatively compatible, we might expect that an older child could draw a younger brother or sister into more advanced symbolic play than a same-age friend, especially during the period in which achieving pretend play with a peer is somewhat problematic. From about twenty-four months of age, most young children can join a same-age peer in social play, and by thirty months such peers often conduct parallel pretend activities, each enacting the same theme, such as putting dolls to bed, and even exchanging smiles and descriptions of what each is doing. But rarely do children of this age coordinate their pretend play so that they take complementary roles and cooperate in developing a single scenario, even though they may be intensely interested in each other's make-believe.[5] Engaging in collaborative action with a peer, simultaneously representing a pretend situation in which two role characters interact, and providing the moment-by-moment communications and metacommunications through which joint pretending is accomplished will only be achieved over the next several months. An older sibling, however, by directing the action and providing the requisite communications, can enlist a younger child in rather complex pretend play, as Judy Dunn and Naomi Dale discovered from their observations in the homes of twenty two-year-olds with their mothers and four- to five-year-old siblings.[6]

The two-year-olds in this study were engaged in play during 21 percent of the observation time and spent about twice as much time playing with their mothers as they did with their older siblings. But play with siblings was quite different in a number of ways. Objects were the pivot for mother-child pretend play: mothers would initiate play by naming or suggesting an action with a replica object; the two-year-olds also engaged mothers in play by bringing them an object. Siblings, however, set up a pretend scenario, transforming locations or identities, and announced at least the beginning of a plan. The children tended to initiate play with older siblings by imitating their actions or by simply moving into the older child's play space, where they would find themselves drafted into a game, assigned a role, or told what to do next. For example, when a two-year-old climbed into a stroller her older sister was pushing, she was designated the baby in a scenario designed by the sibling. Mothers and children rarely enacted complementary roles, while siblings frequently tried to do so with the younger children and occasionally succeeded by using sometimes forceful directions and continuous prompting. Play themes also differed according to the relationship. Siblings enacted everyday routines and household activities with the younger children. With girls mothers more often encouraged or took part in nurturing play using dolls or toy animals. Interestingly, both siblings and mothers initiated play with vehicles only with boys.

The siblings necessarily provided the plan and most of the structure for the coordinated pretend play, and they did so using a variety of communicative techniques. They spoke "in role" and addressed the younger child by role title, made explicit transformations, described ongoing actions, and commented on the characters' feelings and what they would do next. They took responsibility both for the make-believe scenario and for keeping the younger child, who may have been somewhat bewildered from time to time, involved and interested. The four-year-olds were well able to design their comments and questions to enable the younger child to respond, while at the same time advancing the scenario (*Now, are you hungry?* or *You're a little schoolgirl, aren't you?*). With such support, the two-year-olds exhibited more shared pretend play than would have been possible with a same-age peer. The home setting, the presence of familiar toys, and the siblings' history of shared experiences, especially among those who enjoyed an affectionate relationship, were all positive factors in facilitating the younger children's apprenticeship. They may also have learned to play in a somewhat different manner than if their only partners had been their mothers. As the older siblings tried to engineer joint role play, to develop themes that they themselves found appealing, and to design a scenario with appropriate props and settings, they also, inevitably, modeled communicative techniques commonly found in the play of more mature preschoolers. After all, they themselves had probably already learned how preschool peers construct pretend play by playing with their own friends. Their basic problem was to adapt the procedures to include the often willing but unskilled younger child.

The child's first, primary relationships provide an influential context for learning how to play, one that affects the quality and type of play as well as its frequency and duration. Another important factor in how children learn to play is that of the ecology and culture of the community. In groups in which caregiving duties are shared among related adults, siblings, and even young relatives, and in which children themselves are expected to take part in household chores, time for child-centered activities and even objects that are designated as toys may be unavailable—and their absence neither noticed nor missed. Children will make do with materials in the natural environment and use everyday objects in their play when, and if, play is allowed. In fact, the goals and values of many groups may stress the early integration of the child into the work of the extended family. Mothers may have little time to supervise, let alone direct and encourage pretend play, which, in any case, they do not consider an operative factor in development.

Although few detailed observations of the developmental course of pretend play in such communities are available, two studies in small-town or rural agrarian communities in Mexico have noted the rarity of mother-child pretend play and the role of siblings and other young relatives as a child's primary playmates.[7] In such settings, the young child's solitary make-believe play is often ignored and is usually of brief duration. The child participates in social pretend play when enlisted to take some assigned role in the play of older siblings and relatives, who may also be serving as its caregivers. Mixed-age groups often play outdoors, free of close adult supervision. The older children's play will most probably be based on a limited number of routine adult activities, such as cooking or going to the market, rather than on fantastic themes; the roles will be primarily functional or occupational ones, such as shopkeeper, and what few props are used will be natural objects. The young child will be shown and told what to do in order to participate but not encouraged to pursue her own inventions or to add innovative elaborations. Despite these limitations there is no evidence that children's language development or their acquisition of the social knowledge appropriate to their culture suffers thereby. Yet when the play of such children is compared to that of children of the same ages in Western, urban, and technological societies, it appears to be less complex and elaborate.[8] Clearly, the forms and content of pretend play may be pervasively affected by the cultural setting and the abilities and values of children's playmates, whether parents, siblings, or same-age friends. In cultures in which the young child normally plays with a variety of play-mates, the types of play that arise in each grouping generally differ in form, content, and interactional procedures, and each might be expected to support the child's development in some-what complementary ways. The availability, the identity, and the diversity of playmates will also influence the frequency and elaboration of pretend play as well as other kinds of play. Chil-dren's play changes systematically with maturation and cogni-tive growth, but it is also shaped by friends and relations and by the opportunities they variously afford the child to learn the particular styles and procedures that allow her to join in. In a culture in which pretend play is encouraged and believed to be an important factor in development, those children who have had the broadest and most varied assortment of playmates and acquired a flexible repertoire of play styles may have a distinct advantage over those who have had few such opportunities.

PRETEND PLAY: WHAT IS LEARNED

Social pretend play has a number of characteristics that are often used in assessing the maturity of such play and its relation to other aspects of the child's development or social identity. These characteristics include both cognitive, or representational, aspects of pretending and social, or interactional, aspects. Both tend to change over the period during which social pretending flowers, that is, from about three to six or seven years of age. The overall trend is for play to become more collaborative and in-creasingly verbal. Perhaps the most significant insight these char-acteristics reveal, however, is just how complex this kind of play can be and how much preschoolers or children entering kinder-garten must learn in order to enter into such activity. Some of these properties include the following:

1. *PLANNING*.   Pretend activity is internally differentiated. Children often plan in advance what they are going to do, what roles they will assume, what objects or props they will use and how, thus explicitly framing the pretend activity. Even in solitary pretend play, children tend to engage in an initial phase they call "setting up," in which they arrange props and prepare the scene. In social play, children actually enact the pretend scenario after

the initial planning negotiations if these can be worked out to the participants' satisfaction. Without some degree of agreement on role assignment and the overall nature of the plan, however, children either cease to pretend or separate into their individual pretend worlds. Even after the play enactment has begun, there are inevitably changes in plans or problems in the staging that require further communication about the procedures; some of these may briefly interrupt the enactment or force a return to lengthy planning negotiations, while others may be delivered "in role" as the enactment continues. Older children tend to engage in more preplanning and description before enacting a scenario than younger children. Although younger children do assign roles and apportion objects early in the interaction, they rarely delineate a plan for the scenario in advance and often fail to follow through with enactment, perhaps becoming more absorbed in the processes of assigning roles and arranging props. Clearly, advanced planning of a line of action reflects cognitive gains in the ability to conceptualize the direction and the details of an imagined scenario while holding in mind the goal of the action and to coordinate these with another player's image of what is going to unfold.

One type of exchange, which indicates how children represent projected action and monitor the appropriate sequence, can be illustrated as follows. Two boys apportioned the roles of a mechanic, who was at his workshop, and a fireman, whose firetruck had broken down somewhere on the road, and planned how they would handle the problem.* Then, starting the enactment of the scenario, the child playing the mechanic pretended to answer his telephone to take the call for assistance. The child playing the fireman interrupted the mechanic's *Hello, Will-E's Fix-It Shop* by saying, *Wait a minute, I haven't called you yet.* The mechanic realized his error and hung up. The fireman then picked up his phone, simulated dialing, and made a ringing sound. The mechanic answered again, this time on cue, and after hearing about the problem, agreed to send a tow truck. The child playing the fireman presumably had an image of the correct procedure for the opening of the enactment and felt that it was

* I am grateful to Thayer L. Kramer, Department of Psychology, University of Maine, for permission to cite from her transcripts of the play of previously unacquainted preschool children here and on the following pages.

worth the trouble to correct his partner and start again in order to "get it right."

Since planning an episode in advance (or adjusting or correcting some problem during enactment) often involves persuasion and flexibility, social and communicative expertise as well as cognitive ability, is reflected in such exchanges and their successful conclusion. The fireman provided a reason for stopping his partner, and the mechanic was willing to accept the correction and begin again, waiting for the proper signal. Some researchers have suggested that it is the process of negotiation rather than the actual enactment of a scenario through which children achieve the gains in social competence that are associated with peer play. The intricate temporal relationships of planning and enactment, and the fact that children can exchange planning information in subtle ways even as they enact adopted roles, suggest that both functions require interactional and communicative competence if they are to mesh in a successful episode of pretending.

2. *METACOMMUNICATION.* Pretend play displays a wide variety of different verbal and nonverbal techniques, or metacommunications, which convey information about the pretend activities as well as advance them. Although researchers have as yet failed to provide a choreographic notation for children's nonverbal communicative techniques in play, they, and their manner of integration with verbal messages, are as important as talk in the conduct of pretend interactions. Children take several different parts in the production of a pretend episode. They are actors in their adopted roles, but they are also the script writers, directors, and stage managers. At the same time, they are, of course, the real persons who agree to join in the production. These functions are indicated both in speech and in nonverbal behavior.

A variety of verbal message types have been described by Holly Giffin.[9] The types are differentiated by manner of production, by their relation to the type of nonverbal activity (that is, the degree to which nonverbal behavior is consonant with an adopted role or a make-believe activity), and by their function in the management of the activity. The seven types range from "overt proposals" *about* pretend delivered in a normal speaking voice to messages delivered "in role" with vocal modifications appropriate to the character (a gruff voice for Father). In between, and ordered according to the degree to which the pretend frame is exposed or specifically referred to, are a number of subtly different types of messages. "Implicit pretend structuring" is used for planning outside the pretend frame, when children act and speak in their real identities. "Prompting" is a brief interruption in enactment that occurs when one child feeds lines to another or corrects another's performance, usually *sotto voce*. "Story-telling" is used to provide information about the pretend domain, often detailing information about motives or antecedent situations that cannot be depicted nonverbally; it often employs past tense verbs and is sometimes delivered in a sing-song cadence. "Underscoring" is the verbal identification of actions or situations that, realistically speaking, the enacted character would not utter, as when a child says *I'll pour the milk* while nonverbally carrying out the action or announces *I'm crying* in between sobs. "Ulterior conversation," the message type most like pure enactment, is a means by which children, acting in role, provide other characters with suggestions or reports about the ongoing action and thereby advance the plot. For example, a visiting wife commented to her hostess, *Oh, I see you're getting ready to take the baby for a walk* before the mother had even mentioned the idea.

Giffin also noted that children prefer to maintain the pretend illusion whenever possible and thus tend to deliver needed information about changes in plot details or motives for action *within* the pretend frame. Older children are particularly concerned about specifying the personal attributes of pretend characters and their motives and about supplying their partners with background information that informs and justifies current action. Mature play, therefore, is likely to contain more messages that provide a rationale for action but which are slotted into the flow of within-frame communication in order to seem a part of the characters' reasonable talk. Thus, paradoxically, as play becomes more imaginative and fantastic it also becomes more "logical," reasoned, and justified by (pretend) rationalizations. The developmental differences in the type or range of metacommunicative messages children deploy as they become more mature and experienced players and how they fit these messages into sequenced episodes are issues that have yet to be examined in detail in the context of social play.

3. *STRUCTURAL CHANGE.* The basic structural components of pretending—object transformations, decontextualization or the freeing of pretend actions from the constraints of the real setting, actor/role manipulation or the flexible pairings of persons and roles, and the chaining of actions into storylike scenarios—are all subject to developmental change. Again, if the pretending is done socially, there is the added problem of communicating so that plans and transformations are shared. In general, older children are more able to invent imaginary objects or use objects in ways not determined by their real form or function. Object transformations become more "ideational" and less "material," so that the pretend world becomes more elaborately furnished as children grow less dependent on objects provided by others for their play. Similarly, in more mature play the temporal and spatial boundaries of the pretend worlds expand. Children can imagine a broader time frame, incorporating past as well as future events into the make-believe world, and can locate events in more remote settings. Play thus becomes more "fantastic" and less tied to everyday activities such as preparing meals or putting babies to bed. As play becomes more fantastic, more details of the setting must be specified verbally (*tomorrow night, at midnight; way far back in the dark cave*). We have found that children use significantly more temporal and locative adverbs, phrases, and clauses in their pretend play than in their other social interactions, and that older children in particular tend to specify, often rather elaborately, the time and space dimensions of the make-believe setting.[10] Role assignment and adoption also become more varied with age. Older children are not limited to the roles in the nuclear family but can take on those of witches, ghostbusters, lady detectives, and alien monsters. Older children also tend to include more than one type of transformation (object plus role, role plus setting) in a single message, so that their representations of a pretend world, as mirrored in their communications, are more complex. And children's growing ability to construct longer sequences of events is reflected in their more protracted scenarios. Older children tend to spend more time in pretending and develop longer dramas. These developments, however, are related not only to the ability to represent varied and extended imaginative action lines but also to the ability to maintain collaboration with coplayers and to

solve or defuse the inevitable conflicts that arise in social play.

4. *CONFLICT AND NEGOTIATION.* Pretend play is by no means free of opposition and conflict. Older children may have fewer conflicts over the use of an object than younger children, but decided differences of opinion about the details of an imagined world still arise and must be addressed immediately, for shared pretend can only continue if agreement can be assumed. It is not surprising, therefore, that children exert their most sophisticated and persuasive efforts to further pretend play and that they actively work to clarify misunderstandings and misinterpretations. For example, children use more requests for agreement, for compliance, and even for permission when they are engaged in pretend interactions than when they are involved in other social activities. Denials and refusals do occur, but children usually accompany them with reasons, alternative proposals, or suggestions for compromise, or they employ other means for mitigating opposition, such as opening with *Yes, but . . .* , a technique that allows one to seem to accept what the other has said but still to go on to propose an alternative. Their justifications for denying or refusing usually refer to the jointly constructed pretend world so that the players need not abandon their pretend framework while dealing with the disagreement. For example, a five-year-old girl (M) wanted her play partner (E), who was acting as mother, to come to her house but to leave the babies at home; the partner did not want to leave them:

(1) M: You come here. The babies are sleeping now and . . .
    (interrupted).
(2) E: No, they'll cry when I leave 'cause they'll hear the car.
(3) M: Nooo. The car's broken. I have the car.
(4) E: All right, but one baby will have to take care of these little
    babies.

In line 2, E refused M's request but provided a motherly reason for the refusal; in line 3, M denied the possibility of E's reason and explained the grounds for her denial. In line 4, E accepted M's reasoning (her own having been logically faulted) and presumably agreed to *come here* but stipulated a condition that would assure the babies' safety, one with which M agreed. The two children worked all this out without breaching the pretend frame, employing the technique of "ulterior conversation." Impolite, or unmitigated, commands and refusals do occur, even in the best of pretend engagements. As children differentiate between speaking "in role" and negotiating about role-appropriate behavior, an *enacted* character may appropriately shout, *No, I won't!* Or a child speaking as director may issue an abrupt command as required by the action, an order that another child often accepts and executes without challenge.

5. *THEMES AND ISSUES.* The themes of pretend activity range from those of everyday life, such as cooking, shopping, or taking a vacation, to those that are so imaginative and fanciful it would be difficult to trace their components to any particular story or television show. Researchers have distinguished between pretend themes enactive of real life, which draw on relatively familiar event sequences, and more fabulous fantasy themes in which skeletons come to life or cars fly. It has been widely observed that younger children tend to prefer more familiar events, while older children invent more imaginative fantasies. For older children also, an everyday theme may change during the course of play to a more fantastic one. For example, the two boys who were acting as the mechanic and the fireman eventually made a smooth transition from diagnosing a malfunction in the carburetor of the firetruck to fighting off an "Everything-Eating-Lamb" that had gotten into the truck and was devouring its engine.

Greta Fein has suggested that underlying both everyday and fantastic themes are a number of recurring issues that reflect the perennial concerns of childhood and often carry a strong positive or negative affective charge.[11] These issues can be realized in relatively familiar themes or in more imaginative dramas, as in the case of the boys' dramatic escalation from a defective carburetor to an omnivorous lamb. The fundamental issues Fein has postulated are those of attachment (interpersonal affiliation versus separation or rejection), physical well-being (harm versus safety or health), empowerment (mastery versus helplessness or failure), social regulation (compliance with social rules versus transgressions), and respect for physical objects (property protection versus damage). Preschoolers might not recognize the cover terms for these issues, but they must deal with specific instances of each category every day: Mother must be away for a few days; the child inexplicably has a painful earache, is not able to drive the car as an older cousin can, or is punished for hitting a younger sibling; or a favorite teddy bear, left out in the rain, begins to come apart. Further study of the way such issues arise and are dealt with in play would contribute to our understanding of the motive forces that support pretending. It might also help to explain how it is that children agree as well as they do on the way plots may develop and are often able to follow one another's ingenious inventions.

6. *AFFECTIVE DISPLAYS.* Researchers have remarked that pretend play interactions are characterized by a relatively high degree of positive emotion. Closer examination of play bouts, however, reveals that both positive and negative affect displays are common. Children do indeed make eye contact often and smile or giggle, signaling to each other their genuine pleasure in the play or their appreciation of some particular imaginative act or idea, and a high level of engrossment in the dramatic action is common. But displays of simulated negative affects, such as fear, dread, shock, or disgust, are also quite common in the enactment phases of play. These displays employ nonverbal gestures, such as facial and postural expressions of horror or outrage, as well as vocal gestures, such as groans or sighs of exasperation, and may also include verbal messages (*Oh! That's awful!; No! I don't believe it*). In fact, a child may even signal danger or trouble by beginning a replay of a scenario with the announcement, said in a serious voice, *This is gonna be terrible!* Such highly expressive negative displays, which are common in enactment, enhance the children's shared excitement of the pretend experience, and no doubt add dramatic intensity and realism to the action.

7. *RECYCLED EPISODES.* Once children have created a satisfying play episode, they very often play it over and over again. Players may recall a particular episode as a part of their shared interactive history. The participants appear to remember the structure of the scenario, and often even an abbreviated cue suffices to initiate a replay. These phenomena, historicity and cyclicity, attest to the importance of the shared pretend experi-

ence in the players' relationship. Recycled episodes are based on what the players have themselves produced together; thus, they do not require extensive preplanning and can be instigated merely by a signal that identifies the theme to the partner. For example, after having called in a fish to eat up worms that were crawling all around the house and thus successfully terminating a threat, a girl signaled to her play partner that the threat had returned by exclaiming, *Uh oh!* as she pretended to spot a new invasion of worms. Both children then began to try to solve the now familiar problem using the proven method of summoning a fish. Other transitional markers and clear references to prior episodes, such as *Oh, not again!*, or *This time I'll be the mechanic*, or *You were the mother last time* indicate that children recall a play sequence as a complete unit of activity, whose structure is readily available to guide a new engagement. Each child also assumes that the other shares this knowledge so that the sequence can be done again. Clearly, the pretend play episode continues to exist as a potential resource in the real world of the children's relationship.

8. THE PRETEND-REAL BOUNDARY. Finally, if players view pretend episodes as integral units of activity, do they also see them as clearly distinguished from the real world? Do children ever confuse events or individuals from the two domains or fail to locate the boundary between the imagined and the actual? Certainly, even experienced five-year-old pretenders seem to need to reassure themselves, on occasion, that there isn't actually a wolf at the door. The two boys mentioned previously showed only assumed alarm at the threat posed by the "Everything-Eating-Lamb." But when they began a new episode in which they faced a similar threat from ghosts (which were eating the mechanic's tools), one boy stepped out of role for a moment to remind his partner, *And by the way, we're only pretending.* A little later, the other boy commented, *There's no such thing as ghosts* and then resumed his involvement in the play episode, telephoning the Ghostbusters for help.

Especially in the heightened excitement of good fantasy play, children may suddenly feel uneasy and in need of reassurance about matters that in a cooler moment they would probably judge as "just make-believe" or "not real." There is, however, a de-

velopmental change both in children's ability to differentiate between reality and fantasy and in the way they deal with real
events that might breach the boundary separating the real and
the pretend world. Lisabeth Fisher DiLalla and Malcolm Watson
studied this change over the age range 2:6 to 6:6 by injecting
interruptions into the fantasy play conducted by the investigator
and a child.[12] The two played superheroes who, to rescue a doll,
must hide from an alien monster, then seek it out and destroy it.
One interruption was external to the plot: at a (real) knock on the
door, the experimenter left the room for a minute. Two were
internal to the story: the adult suggested changing a pretend
tower (actually a table) to a cave; and the adult suddenly changed
roles, from a superhero to the very monster the two superheroes
were hunting. For children between the ages of two and five,
reactions to these interruptions shifted from being unable to continue the fantasy at all, to being a little confused about what was
going on, to dealing with the interruptions by stepping outside
the pretend frame; that is, by using overt proposals or implicit
pretend structuring, they indicated that they perceived a rigid
boundary between the fantasy world and the real world. The
six-year-olds, however, were able to handle the interruptions
from within the pretend frame, weaving them smoothly into the
fantastic plot without stepping out of character. After the play
episode, when children were asked questions about what had
happened (*Were you really Superman?* and *Were you afraid of the
monster? Why or why not?*), their answers paralleled their previous reactions to the interruptions. Thus, a six-year-old child talking about the game stated that he had only been pretending and
that pretend is "not really being it" since superheroes are not
real. During play, when faced with the experimenter's suggestion that the tower become a cave, this child had said *Poof! I will
use my superpowers to turn this tower into a cave!*

With the growing ability to distinguish cognitively fantasy or
fiction from reality in a number of different content areas, children are also better able to identify or localize the negative affect
that may accompany intense imagining. They can recognize,
even explore, distressing ideas or feelings within the play frame
with increasingly less likelihood that these ideas or feelings will
permeate the boundary of the imagined and the actual worlds.
Children are also learning the interactive procedures and meta-

communicative techniques through which they can flexibly handle problems, conflicts, and other unexpected events within the pretend frame and even integrate them into the text or plot in order to maintain the flow of social pretend activity.

The episodic structure of play engagements, whether recycled or newly constructed, can provide measures of imaginative maturity and successful interaction. Coherent episodes and the smooth development of themes within episodes (as opposed to rapid shifting of themes and a failure to develop any particular theme) are characteristic of older or more mature players. These children are familiar with conventional signals and appropriate types of messages that variously facilitate episode construction, and they can link episodes into protracted dramas. Older children do, indeed, produce proportionally more pretend utterances than younger children, but of greater significance is the fact that their pretend utterances tend to occur in more conversationally coherent sequences. Players jointly develop plots as they actually take turns speaking, sometimes even building on one another's sentence structures. The two boys, who had failed by themselves to vanquish the "Everything-Eating-Lamb," decided to call the police for help. As the fireman (F) finished telephoning the police, the mechanic (M) made a suggestion:

(1) M: Yeah, you should have called Inspector Gadgen . . . um hum.
(2) F: And Chief Quimby.
(3) M: Um well . . . Chief Quimby . . . well, Chief Quimby actually tells Inspector Gadgen . . . (interrupted).
(4) F: Yeah, but he also calls to give him an assignment . . . too.
(5) M: Okay . . . you . . . okay, you're gonna be Chief Quimby . . . okay?

In this sequence, the children worked out a minor difference of opinion, which they had to address before they could resume their enactment of the attempt to summon help. In doing so, they jointly built complex sentence structures (*You should have called Inspector Gadgen . . . and Chief Quimby. Chief Quimby actually tells Inspector Gadgen . . . but he also calls to give him an assignment*). They also made some effort to sustain (or appear to sustain) agreement while working out this difference. They both mitigated the form of disagreement (using *yeah* before criticizing as in line 1; beginning a disagreement with *well*, as in line 3 and *yeah but . . .* as in line 4) and either acknowledged the other's contribution (*too* in line 4) or checked to be sure the other concurred (the final *okay?* of line 5). At the same time, they were mutually responsible for advancing the plot by substituting Inspector Gadgen and then Chief Quimby for the anonymous police, by characterizing the new pretend roles, and by achieving the transformation of the fireman in the previous play sequence to Chief Quimby. While the children were using their knowledge of conversational structure and the conventions of polite, or at least reasonably tactful, social interaction, they were also employing specialized techniques for constructing pretend activity, techniques that they had mastered during the course of numerous previous social play engagements.

10/ Play and the Real World

The child's experiences in the real world provide the resources for play. Objects and their properties, the possibility of locomotion and of increasingly skilled coordination, the resources of language and communication, the intriguing complexities of social role relationships and dramatic plots, and the challenge of limits, rules, and conventions are among the raw materials that the child can exploit. But the real world impinges on the child's play in other, more direct ways. Aspects of the child's social identity—sex, cultural setting, and family and community organization, values, and beliefs—will influence the style, kinds, and amount of play a child will display. In inner-city communities where black English is spoken, for example, certain styles of verbal play are commonly practiced and highly valued. Such play involves both play with language and provocative play with social conventions. Individual social standing in part depends on the command of these highly structured types of repartee and the ability to "keep cool" while giving and receiving outrageous insults or challenges to self-esteem. Young children in such communities gradually learn this style of verbal play, using one-liners at first, but often accidentally giving or taking real offense before they understand how to use the techniques creatively and with the proper emotional distance.[1]

A further example of the influence of family and culture on children concerns the amount and type of fantasy expression that is tolerated, encouraged, or allowed to arise within the social settings of a cultural group. Shirley Brice Heath has described how imaginative stories or elaborations of real events may be supported in one socioeconomic or ethnic group, while similar make-believe accounts may be judged as lying and are negatively sanctioned in another group.[2] She suggests that these conventions for handling fact and fiction may also have repercussions in children's successful adaptation to the demands of formal schooling. A similar account of culturally based differences in the appearance of social make-believe play is reported by Shlomo Ariel and Irene Sever, who contrasted Sinai Bedouin children in a traditional community with children in a "western" social group living in a kibbutz.[3] The Bedouin children, who had very little playful interaction with adults and received no formal instruction, exhibited little pretend play, but the children in the kibbutz, who spent a lot of time with adults, attended kindergarten, and were often read fairy tales and stories, did play imaginatively using both everyday and fictional or fantastic themes. Thus, play can vary in quite radical and systematic ways according to the differences in the attitudes, values, and child-rearing practices of the communities to which children belong.

The child's own disposition, health, and competencies will also be reflected in play behavior. Since there are many different kinds of play, each of which may derive from and support different aspects of the child's personality and developing capabilities, efforts to identify a generalized, stable trait of "playfulness" have not as yet been highly successful. Yet teachers and other habitual observers of children have noted differences among preschool peers in their expression of positive affect, the imaginativeness of their pretend inventions, their whole-hearted engagement in pretend activities, and the success with which they sustain play interactions, characteristics that may be related to important differences in children's status in the peer group (a topic that will be discussed later in this chapter). It has been possible to identify some preferences in play styles as children move into the period of symbolic representation. Some children, who have been called "dramatists," prefer to engage in play with a narrative dimension and tend to use objects to support social roles and story lines. Other children, the "patterners," are interested in the physical properties of objects and in their possible combinations and arrangements. After the age of three, both types of children become more versatile, engaging in both types of activities but still showing some evidences of their prior preferences.[4]

Age and level of sociocognitive maturity are, of course, powerful influences on the types and varieties of children's play, as we have seen in previous chapters. In particular, the sequence of developmental changes in early symbolic play (described in Chapter 4) is sufficiently regular and predictable that pronounced deviations can be used to understand developmental problems in specific areas. A particularly striking example is that of childhood autism. Unlike children suffering from Down's syndrome, autistic children do not engage in pretend play or share in pretense with others, although they are members of cultural groups in which pretend play is modeled and valued. This observation along with subsequent studies led Alan Leslie to propose a specific deficit in cognitive processing in such children, one that also underlies their inability to attribute to others (or to themselves) such mental states as *believe, think, know,* or *guess,* or to make and understand such statements as *he's just pretending* or *it isn't really a bottle.*[5] In contrast, the normal three-year-old does distinguish in the course of her play between what something "really" is and what it will temporarily count as in her pretend world. She understands the revocability of pretend transformations (although she may not be able to express that understanding in so many words), and she usually recognizes that she can act in the realm of the actual world or step at will into the realm of an imaginary world. Furthermore, she assumes that a play partner can and will make the same distinctions and will try when necessary to clear up discrepancies in their individual understanding of a play sequence, pointing out what is "really real" or what is "just make-believe." The child has, in effect, begun to develop a theory of mind by realizing that there can be different mental models of the world, and that a state of affairs can be known, pretended, or hoped to be the case. She may stand squarely in the "paramount reality of everyday life," but she will become increasingly flexible over the next several years in operating on other worlds and with other people's experience of other worlds, an area and direction of growth not open to the autistic child.

Of the many diverse relationships between play and the real world, we will select three for further discussion, all of which are of current theoretical and practical concern because of their implications in children's lives. The first is the relation of gender to play; the second the relation of play to children's social status and friendship; and the third the relation of play to narrative ability and other competencies associated with the development of literacy. Although developmentalists have devoted extensive research to children's understanding of gender roles and their gender-differentiated behavior, to the nature and importance of peer relationships in childhood, and to how children comprehend written texts and how they learn to read, investigation of the role of play in these critical areas of development is relatively new.

GENDER VARIATIONS IN PLAY

Decided preferences for sex-stereotypic toys and activities begin to appear during the child's second year of life. This is hardly surprising, since parents and relatives consistently provide sex-appropriate toys, clothing, room furnishings, and entertainment. More extensive experience with agemates, in daycare or nursery school, amplifies the child's sex-appropriate preferences and behaviors. By elementary school age, sex segregation and specialization is the norm in most kinds of play as well as in other activities. Despite differences in the values and organization of diverse communities and cultures, these tendencies are virtually universal. Children generally play in same-sex groupings, in childhood a "best friend" is usually of the same sex, and those who have imaginary playmates even tend to create them in their own image. The current trend toward women's increasing participation in various occupations and recreational activities previously reserved for men appears to have had rather negligible effects as yet on children's choice of toys or play activities. According to some researchers, educators, and parents' organizations, the goal of "equal opportunity" cannot be achieved without equal abilities and skills. There is therefore some concern that sex segregation and same-sex specialization in play, along with other types of peer interactions, may afford boys and girls quite different experiences of the physical and social worlds and thereby affect their general profile of skills, interests, expectations, and achievement goals.

Mixed-sex groupings can, of course, be encouraged through the intentional curricular and environmental engineering of caregivers and teachers. But mixed-sex interactions, even friendships, during the preschool and elementary school period are not unusual, although they are more likely to be found in small neighborhood groups. For the most part, however, girls play with girls and boys with boys, especially in school settings. These associations support and magnify any existing preferences for sex-appropriate toys, play activities, and games, and provide additional conventions for distinguishing between how girls and boys behave. Peers assure the observance of the local norms by teasing, taunting, and even rejecting the child who fails to conform. Boys are somewhat more "at risk" for exhibiting an interest in dolls or for joining girls in the household play corner or at their specialized games than are girls who show an interest in vehicles, space-age weapons, or boys' construction activities and sports. Teachers are also more likely to approve girls' cross-sex behavior. A boy or girl who attempts to enter a sex-segregated area on a playground or to join an activity in that community that is specialized by sex invites a "put down" that invokes the unique rights, knowledge, and abilities of the proprietary sex. For example, three boys who were building a fort were observed to react to a girl's approach by saying *Go away. We don't want girls here.* Likewise, a group of girls refused a boy's offer to swing one end of a jump rope: *You can't play. You don't know how to swing it. You gotta be a girl.*

Either sex can recognize and sanction inappropriate behavior on the part of its own members and those of the opposite sex— this is a natural consequence of learning one's own gender role. In fact, knowledge of the role behavior, preferences, and expectations of the opposite gender in part defines the boundaries of the gender identity of the self. Nor is there any doubt that children are willing co-conspirators in constructing the complex attitudes and behavior of gender identity and the patterns of sex-stereotyping. In an interesting report on gender arrangements in a large and diverse sample of elementary schools, Barrie Thorne has described a number of conventions and interaction rituals by which children both affirm their own identity in single-sex groupings and perpetuate accepted stereotypes.[6] These include contests between a boys' side and a girls' side; "rituals of pollution" in which one sex (usually male) is contaminated by the touch of the other sex (usually female); "invasions" in which (usually) boys tease or otherwise disrupt girls' games; and cross-sex chasing. Thorne recounts an incident that shows just how aware children are of these attitudes and patterns of behavior. "I watched a second grade boy teach a kindergarten girl how to chase. He ran slowly backwards, beckoning her to pursue him, as he called, 'Help, a girl's after me.' "

The well-known facts are that, compared with most girls, most boys are on the whole more boisterous, energetic, and noisy; contact more different companions and interact with them more briefly; cover more physical space and keep a greater distance from teachers or adult supervisors; and are more quarrelsome and competitive. They are also generally judged to be more assertive and independent, and to more often display individual initiative.* These tendencies are especially obvious in outdoor play, in play with motion and interaction, especially physical contact play, and in the selection of favorite games. But to what extent do these tendencies influence pretend play? Recent investigations have pursued this issue beyond the ubiquitous observation that boys prefer to adopt the roles of powerful superheroes engaged in daring actions, fighting, or killing, and girls those of family members engaged in more routine and nurturant activities. An important question is whether boys' and girls' social pretend play differs primarily in terms of the type of transformational components they employ ("material," or concrete, versus "ideational," or abstract object transformations), which are generally assumed to index the cognitive complexity and maturity of make-believe play, or in terms of the communicative components and styles of interpersonal interaction they demonstrate during play.

As children develop they tend to add ideational object transformations to their earlier concrete object substitutions. They also begin to add fictitious characters and fantastic themes to their previous repertoire of nuclear family roles and everyday themes. As their props and themes become less dependent on perceptible objects and familiar events, they communicate more about their play, in part because less information about the pretend worlds can be obtained from the real-life setting. In actual

---

* Researchers do generalize about boys as a group and girls as a group. It is useful, however, to consider that we are referring to what in our culture is conventionally designated as boylike and girllike behavior, and that any individual may exhibit a mixture of both.

practice, therefore, the cognitive and communicative aspects of social pretending might be expected to interact and may thus be difficult to disentangle. At the same time, many boys and girls do seem to have somewhat different social and personal goals in their nonpretend interactions; for example, harmonious or, at least, noncompetitive interpersonal relationships may be more important to girls than to boys. We might expect that such goals would influence the conduct of children's pretend activities as well as of their games and sports. If girls value harmonious relations, they may choose themes for pretend play that are familiar to all the participants, thus reducing the likelihood of arguments about rules and procedures. And if girls prefer more sedentary activities or intimate social talk, they may choose to have a tea party or put babies to bed rather than to chase escaping bandits or fight off invaders from outer space. Identifying the relative contributions of cognitive, communicative, and interactional goals in the pretend play of boys and girls and determining the influence of differing styles in achieving them will obviously be a difficult task.

Observing the interactions of three- and four-year-olds in same-sex groups of three, Betty Black found that boys were indeed more likely than girls to generate pretend themes completely unrelated to props in the room and that older boys especially generated fanciful themes for play.[7] In addition, boys were more likely than girls to enact their themes in pretend play, while girls were more likely to describe and plan their play. Younger children as a group also did more describing and planning that was not followed through with enactment. Thus, boys' play might seem to display some of the characteristics that are associated with greater cognitive maturity in play. When engaged in planning and describing pretend play, however, girls' talk was more topically coherent, as were their nonpretend conversations, a finding that suggests greater communicative competence (and perhaps more attentiveness to their partner's speech) on the part of girls. Boys tended to produce fewer episodes of topically coherent talk either in their nonpretend interactions or in describing or making plans for pretend play, and they engaged in more solitary pretense than girls. Boys tended more frequently to switch from one pretend topic to another, and often one boy would try to impose his own new pretend plan on the ongoing play interaction of the other boys. These findings suggest that boys may be less concerned with maintaining collaborative group activity and more concerned with pursuing their own individual interests. It has been noted in other studies that boys tend to talk, each about his own pretend activities or plans. In *enacting* pretense, however, the boys and girls in Black's study were similar in respect to their production of topically coherent exchanges: once they agreed upon a plan, both sexes appeared able to pursue it collaboratively. It could be the case, of course, that switching topics frequently or selecting a solitary pretend activity are ways in which boys try to avoid or disengage from conflict in the course of organizing joint pretend activity.

Although some studies have found that boys tend to engage in more social pretend play than girls, other studies have reversed these findings. Jennifer Connolly, Anna Beth Doyle, and Flavia Cheschin compared boys' and girls' pretend play by observing four- and five-year-olds interacting in groups in a nursery school.[8] They found no sex differences in the amount of social pretend play, but the older children, as would be expected, engaged in more social pretend than the younger ones. Also, older children produced more play episodes containing more than one transformation, although there was no difference between boys and girls on this measure of cognitive complexity. Boys did adopt character roles and used substitute objects (such as a toy iron for a gun) more often than girls, who preferred familial roles and used replica objects (such as a toy iron for the pretend action of ironing). But the fact that *older* children adopted functional roles more often than younger ones and used more replicas than substitutes raises the possibility that older children's choices are not so much constrained by cognitive limitations as they are influenced by their preference for certain types of activities. They choose themes compatible with their physical activity interests, interpersonal goals, and self-image, and with the social organization of the participants; that is, an older child, boy or girl, has the cognitive ability necessary to pretend with either replicas or substitute objects (or with completely imaginary objects), but he or she will tend to make the type of transformation that is necessary to carry out the desired plan of action, using for example, a replica iron if it is handy and the mother needs to iron a dress for the baby. If the child sees himself as an intrepid and invincible hero who needs to shoot an invading space monster, and no replica gun is available (as is often the case in playrooms furnished by adults), he might use a hand and finger, a toy screwdriver, or a baby bottle as a gun. In order to test this hypothesis, it would be necessary to examine how children develop an action plan in their moment-by-moment exchanges and to follow the order in which they introduce pretend components when different types of objects are available.

Connolly and her associates then asked whether the observed differences in the frequency and complexity of children's social play (both of which differed by age) were related to their social competence. The children's social competence had previously been assessed using observations of nonpretend social interactions, teacher ranking of peer status and of successful interactions with peers, and measures of social role taking. The important result of their analysis was that for both girls and boys, the two measures of maturity in pretend play were highly related to the measures of social competence. Furthermore, sex-related differences in pretend role preferences and object transformations were indirectly related to social competence. It may be that girls who tend to adopt functional and character roles as well as familial roles and use substitute objects as well as replicas acquire more varied experience of both the physical and interpersonal worlds and are then seen as more flexible and socially competent.

Although differences in the cognitive capabilities displayed by boys and girls in their pretend play have not been demonstrated, the fact still remains that they do go about pretend play in somewhat different ways, and that these different communicative and interactional styles may reflect real differences in the personal and interactive goals of the two sexes. Certainly, boys are generally observed to engage in more conflict than girls, often over choice of role—boys are more likely to insist on adopting a "high-status" role—or as a result of their insisting on a particular action plan rather than accepting a compromise. Girls are more likely to propose pretend transformations in more "polite" language. In opposing another player or pursuing a conflict, boys are more likely to use "heavy-handed persuasion" techniques to get their way and less likely to use mitigated persuasion, and these tendencies are consistent whether the partner is a boy or a girl.

Girls, however, are more flexible; they tend to be more conciliatory with other girls but can be quite directly confrontational with a boy. There is no question that most girls command the verbal techniques for "heavy-handed" persuasion; in enacting role relationships in which peremptory orders, aggravated refusals, and angry responses are appropriate, they are able to use these as the scenario demands.

In fact, research on sex differences in play has focused on profiling the behavior of boys as a group and of girls as a group. It has as yet failed to pursue any of the interesting questions about the range and versatility of children's play behavior or the conditions under which children might demonstrate flexibility in the cognitive and communicative aspects of make-believe or other types of play. Nor have the influences of group size and composition, of a child's prior experience with social pretend play, or of the setting and the behavior of adults in the setting on gender-related differences in children's play behavior been extensively explored.

It should be noted that many boys are also able to use mitigated persuasion techniques. Especially in compatible pairs or dyads who have "hit it off" (whether a girl and boy or two boys), boys are able to compromise with the partner's proposals, use polite requests, and diffuse differences in opinions or desires by offering acceptable justifications and reasons. Boys are also able to engage in lengthy pretend interactions on a single shared theme and use a variety of metacommunicative techniques at appropriate points in the interaction. A major factor in their success may be the strength of their desire to maintain the pretend interaction and to preserve the compatible interpersonal relationship that generally underlies such highly successful pretend engagements.

FRIENDSHIP AND OTHER PEER RELATIONSHIPS

It is as true for the adult as for the three-year-old: if there is something you like to do and some particular person you enjoy doing it with, then you probably consider that person a friend. Of course, as children develop, their concept of friendship enlarges to include ideas such as loyalty, trust, mutual understanding, and intimacy, but playing together and sharing nonplay activities remain salient properties of friendship. In the preschool period, friends and favorite playmates are nearly synonymous. It is not surprising that the quality and quantity of children's play with each other varies according to the nature of their social relationships. Joining in the play of others and sharing playtime are central to children's social relationships; not having anyone to play with when others are engaged with their companions is a serious and sad state of affairs. In this section we will explore the relation between play activities and familiarity, friendship, and peer status, that is, the degree to which a child is accepted and liked by his associates.

Familiarity is undoubtedly a major influence on the quality and quantity of children's play. For the most part, children prefer to play with those they know and seem to be able to achieve more engrossing and successful play episodes with familiar peers than with strangers. Even toddlers exhibit more mutual imitation and more positive interaction with toys and show more complex object play if they play with a familiar child than if they are paired with an unfamiliar child. With a known playmate, the cautious exploration often required to get to know a new person is unnecessary, and familiars may already have shared play preferences and experiences on which they can build new interactions. At three years of age, children interact differently when paired with familiars than they do when paired with strangers. Anna Beth Doyle and her associates reported that the acquainted pairs they observed engaged in more associative and cooperative play and more dramatic or pretend play than stranger pairs; stranger pairs showed more solitary or onlooking behavior than the familiar pairs and engaged in virtually no dramatic play.[9] In addition, familiars displayed many more peer-directed social behaviors, and more of these were positive and interactionally effective, such as following a partner's initiation of a play episode.

Friendship, even in the preschool period, is something more than just familiarity. Although friendships tend to be more stable in the later elementary school years, and some become quite strong as children approach adolescence and have a real "chum," even kindergartners may be said to have friends—people they usually prefer to be with and miss when they are separated from. Being a friend confers a special, privileged status. Children often use the term instrumentally to gain access to the ongoing play of others, reminding a prospective playmate: *We're friends, right?* They also use the term to control a recalcitrant playmate (*If you don't let me have a turn, I won't be your friend anymore*). "Real" friends, however, display their special relationship in a number of ways. In kindergarten classes or play groups, friends naturally gravitate toward each other and may have special play routines they never tire of repeating. Catherine Emihovich described one such set of friends.[10] Unlike the other children in the class, these three (a girl and two boys) always addressed each other by name except during pretend enactment, when they used their role names, and each child always took the same role every time they "played house." Other children in the class recognized the exclusivity of this group and rarely attempted to intrude on the friends' interaction. In play activities in which there is some risk of danger, such as rough and tumble contact play, children also prefer to play with friends, presumably because they are more familiar with each other's play signals and assume that in case they do accidentally inflict some hurt, the friend is less likely to reciprocate in real anger.

The processes through which children become friends and some of the characteristics of this evolving relationship have been investigated by John Gottman and his students in several longitudinal studies.[11] During early childhood, children's principal task in the process of becoming friends is to achieve interpersonal coordination. This task is achieved through mutually entertaining and enjoyable play. Children tend, in any interaction, to try to escalate the level of mutual responsiveness, moving toward play that demands greater interpersonal understanding and reciprocity. We would agree with Gottman that the highest level of coordinated play is fantasy play; it cannot be achieved without continuous interpersonal monitoring, clear and appropriate communication, whole-hearted involvement, and a willingness to compromise. In fantasy play, Gottman believes, children can learn to manage emotional arousal, and when they engage in such play with friends they can sometimes reveal, albeit indirectly, matters of intimate emotional concern—issues similar to those proposed by Greta Fein (see Chapter Nine). Fantasy play, as we have noted, is subject to frequent disputes, but pairs of friends differ from nonfriends in their willingness to drop, gloss over, or resolve opposition. Friends display a higher ratio of agreements (defined as positive or supportive statements) to disagreements (defined as uncooperative or critical statements) not only in fantasy play, but also in other interactions. Quite common in the play of young friends are such exchanges as these: *I'm putting my baby to bed.* / *I'm putting my baby to bed, too* and *I'm gonna grow up and be a policeman.* / *Me, too, 'cause that's what I wanna be when I grow up.* Friends are concerned about discovering and expressing commonalities. Some researchers have also commented on the frequency of *let's* and *we* expressions in friends' conversations (*We're having a good time, aren't we?*). As children approach middle childhood, the importance of fantasy play in friendship formation and maintenance diminishes, and other processes, such as comparing talents or experiences, gossip, and exploration of differences in tastes and interests assume more central roles.

Having a good friend or friends tends to enhance a child's social status in his peer group, but popularity is very different from friendship. Popularity, or the lack of it, reflects the assessments of others. Researchers agree that children who are rejected or actually disliked by their peer group may have trouble achieving successful social adaptation. Researchers and other children alike usually regard these children as disruptive and aggressive. They will be avoided, and their noisy or hostile attempts to get attention or gain access to the activities of others will only exacerbate their rejected status, which unfortunately remains rather stable, not only during childhood but into adolescence. The result, of course, is that they do not have the opportunity to play or otherwise successfully interact with their peers. Children who may not be actively disliked but who are nonetheless excluded from the group—or are rarely incorporated into group play—also lack such opportunities. These children, called "isolates" or neglected children, spend more time unoccupied or as onlookers than normal children and rarely enter into rough and tumble games or group dramatic play; when they do pretend, their play is likely to be solitary. They are relegated to the status of perennial stranger in the group. Thus, aggressive behavior or even immature play behavior contributes to unpopularity and hinders access to the play, games, and conversations of other children, although additional factors such as physical unattractiveness or an unusual name may also have a negative affect on a child's social status.

Popular children are seen as leaders in the group. As might be expected, they tend not to get into fights, are neither hostile nor aggressive, and their behavior is generally cooperative and appropriate in classroom or playground settings. We might suspect that they are skilled and imaginative playmates, since children who are fluent in play are generally liked. Two studies have provided more detail about what popular, or liked, children actually do that gains the esteem of their group.[12] Both studies used a "critical event" technique: a room was set up so that one child had to join the ongoing play of two other children, a situation that frequently occurs in classrooms and play groups. The way the child attempted to gain entry to the play and coped with the usually less than welcoming responses of the constituted group revealed critical information about his social competence and adaptivity.

The two studies together provide the following picture of the liked child, which is a mirror image of the disliked, or rejected, child. First, the popular child does not try to disrupt the other children's play and is sensitive to what they are doing; he does not try to draw attention to himself, but rather makes relevant comments on the group's current activity. In order to do this, of course, he must pay attention, accurately infer just what might be the frame of reference of the group (that is, Are they joking? Are they pretending? What are they pretending?), and adopt that frame of reference himself. Only then can he successfully join the group, entering relatively unobtrusively. Second, he communicates clearly, responsively, and relevantly. He speaks directly to both members of the group, positively acknowledges what others say, and if he must disagree, provides a reason, an alternative suggestion, or a compromise, rather than just a bare "no." Being attentive to the purpose at hand and responsive to others, contributing positively to the ongoing action, and communicating clearly and relevantly are characteristic of both popular children and those who are skilled practitioners of pretend play during early childhood. These interactional skills, however, do not naturally diminish as pretend play is gradually replaced with other types of peer engagements; rather, they are readily generalizable to other types of interactions and social tasks, tending to be as stable as is the child's status with his peers, to which they continue to contribute. The popular child tends to elicit positive responses from peers, often without any apparent effort, and thereby gains even more experience in initiating and extending positive and enjoyable social interactions.

PLAY, NARRATIVE, AND LITERACY

As a child becomes capable of symbolic representation, both language and symbolic play develop rapidly, reflecting the impulse to organize and order experience. As early as two years of age, a child's play actions with dolls and replica objects (feeding a doll, putting it to bed, covering it up) reveal a concern with the orderly sequencing of familiar events. The action is often accompanied by a step-by-step verbal account of the action. At about the same time, the child also begins to express verbally an interest in the way things generally happen in the everyday world as well as remembering past events and anticipating future events.[13] Personal experiences have now become a topic for thought, and they are embodied in the stories the child produces, not only with conversational support from a caregiver but even when alone. In fact, when alone and free of the constraints of conversation or the need to persuade or reply to another person, a child may actually produce more complex, varied, and extended texts than during interaction with caregivers, if the child has already begun to use language to "think" aloud. Storytelling, like pretend play, provides a way to capture, recapture, and foresee or "prescript," experience, even invent it. Telling stories about routine events, anticipated events, and remembered events continues to evolve over the preschool years, enriched by the child's linguistic development and by her increasing knowledge of the uses and varied styles of story-telling.

Children's stories, both those they tell themselves and those they tell others, reveal a growing sophistication about how to create texts. Texts require decontextualized, or relatively autonomous, uses of language, so that understanding a text does not depend directly on the immediate environment of the listener or reader. A parallel development is apparent in more mature pretend play, which is augmented by transformations and story lines that are less dependent on objects in the immediate setting. In addition, texts, like pretend play, are bounded or framed as distinct, independent entities. The competent reader or writer does not confuse the real and the fictional, just as the skilled pretender distinguishes the make-believe world from the real world and protects it from disruptions or intrusions. Eventually, of course, the child must learn to create many different kinds of written and oral texts and learn to understand and produce the sometimes decontextualized language he will encounter in school. Story-telling (and, of course, listening to stories) and pretend play are among the diverse experiences that contribute, in the first several years of life, to the future achievement of literacy.

Narrative is only one kind of story structure, but it is a very important one. Narrative has been defined as "the symbolic presentation of a sequence of events connected by subject matter and related by time."[14] Narratives are essentially accounts of past events that are related through plot, that is, are interpretable according to causes, contingencies, and outcomes. The subject matter of the narrative usually derives from some remarkable event—something unusual or unexpected, something that posed a problem to be solved or a difficulty to be overcome. Even within the limits of this category of text, the child approaching school age commands an amazing variety of types of narrative. Although many researchers have limited their inquiry to children's production of original fantasy narratives or to their understanding of stories selected from children's literature, many other distinct types of narrative are more commonly created in children's spontaneous talk.

It is not surprising that five-year-olds have already discovered many ways to use narrative in naturally occurring social interactions. It can be used to report a personal experience or something of interest that happened to family or friends; to "snitch on," complain about, or inform on another person; to explore a hypothetical situation (*What if?*); or to fool another person into accepting fiction as fact. It can also be used purely as entertainment or for mutual fun. And, since few things we do or say have only one purpose, a story that reports a personal experience can be designed to show the teller in a favorable light while at the same time disparaging another character. What is surprising, however, is that children of this age can distinguish a number of different styles and categories of narrative in their own oral creations. Alison Preece recorded the spontaneous conversations of three five-year-olds whom she drove in a car pool to and from school over a period of eighteen months.[15] In all, the children produced fourteen different types of narrative, the typology being based not only on the source and content of the tale but also on the distinctive techniques used for framing and structuring the varieties and the styles of verbal production. One type, for example, the "original fantasy," was always introduced by a conventional opener, such as *once upon a time,* and closed with *the end*; it included fantasy characters who confronted challenges or dilemmas. In most of the children's narrative performances, one person was the chief narrator, although the "audience" generally contributed appreciation or criticism of the performance, sometimes helped out with prompts, and sometimes displayed evidence of disbelief. A number of imaginative stories were produced collaboratively by two or all three of the children, and they sometimes planned the performance before actually beginning. All three children were adept at launching a narrative into the stream of conversation and marking it as a boundaried whole, distinct from the surrounding talk. Conversational interaction, of course, is the natural environment for most of the stories that both children and adults hear and produce.

The most common type of narrative for these children, as for most adults, was the "personal anecdote" introduced by the irresistible question, *Know what happened to me?* or *Guess what!,* or by some other attention-getter that informs the addressee that an anecdote is imminent. Second in frequency was the "anecdote of vicarious experience," a story about something notable that happened to someone else. This, like personal anecdote, is also very common in adult talk. Three other types distinguished by the children were distinctly playful. The most popular of these was the "narrative parody," a story whose style and content either mocked the story or the process of story-telling itself. True to a basic rule of play, once you have learned to do something the "right" way, you can then proceed to take liberties with its form or function. Also popular was the "con," a narrative set forth as a true account and only exposed as a fiction when the audience finally woke up to the trick. A third playful type was called the "narrative joke," which was based on what was apparently seen as a humorous event. Children of this age can be amused merely by recognizing that something is incongruous and do not require that the incongruity be resolved or that verbal ambiguity be appreciated, as is generally the case for adults. Thus, these rather simple narrative jokes would probably seem funny only to the children themselves.

Material deriving from movies or TV and perceived by the teller as either funny or scary formed the basis for one type of "retelling" narrative, but it was not as coherently structured and by no means as lengthy as retellings from print sources, fairy tales, or other stories that the children had heard read to them. These retellings contained many of the literary devices of their originals, including numerous direct quotations from the original sources, which indicates that stories read to children provide an influential model for their own "literary" text constructions. Even three-year-olds inventing their own fictional stories know that one must begin with *once upon a time* and conclude with *the end*.

One other popular type of narrative Preece recorded was the hypothetical or "What-if?" narrative. Not limited to an account of past events, this type dealt with what might happen or what would or could have happened, although the events in the hypothetical scenario were mentioned in the order of their (projected) occurrence. These productions were often collaborative; the first narrator would introduce an imagined problem situation and the co-narrators would then propose solutions or further complications that would foil a suggested solution. The "What-if?" narrative unfolds in ways similar to some of the planning negotiations that occur in social pretend play in which children challenge a proposed transformation or action line, giving make-believe reasons for why an alternative transformation or plan is required. For example, *You can't come with me. You have to stay at home and take care of the babies. / But, you 'sposed to be the doctor that takes care of the babies.* This brief description of the spontaneous narratives of three young children complements and extends other research that stresses the importance of conversation as a context in which narrative types and functions are differentiated and in which narrative structure and some aspects of text-forming language develop.

The full structure of completely developed narrative is quite complex, and in conversation not all of the possible components are consistently present, even in adult talk. But by the age of five or six children tend to provide not only the essential core of the narrative, the complication (that is, the ordered events or "what happened"), but may also precede it with an introduction, often with an abstract of the story to be told and some indication of time, location, relevant objects, and characters.[16] Following the complication, the child may describe her attitude or reaction to the events, or at least indicate the result or outcome of the events. And finally, the speaker and the listener must return from narrative time to the real time of the present conversation, but this transition need not be, and often is not, explicitly indicated.

The similarity between the structure of narrative and the structure of relatively mature social pretend play is obvious. In the latter, too, participants are introduced into the pretend frame (*Let's play house*). They then provide information about setting (*This is our living room. / Yeah, and pretend it was evening so we had to fix dinner.*). Next they experience a sequence of ordered events, often ones that provide a challenge or problem, such as discovering a fire in the kitchen, which also suggests the objective of putting it out. Evaluative reactions to the events are common (*Wow, that was terrible!*), and often a result or outcome is provided (*Well, it's safe to go to bed now. / Yeah, goodnight.*). Also, little narratives, usually truncated in structure, are often embedded in the pretend play. One function of such embedding appears to be to give necessary background information for a new activity, that is, to furnish an explanation to a partner of why some action is required. When one five-year-old boy called the "police fixing department," he explained at some length to the mechanic (his partner) what had happened using an ordered sequence of narrative clauses but interspersing these with other vital descriptive information: *Well, my truck is broken down. It crashed again. It jammed into another car . . . another car was coming this way and my fire engine was coming this way and I jammed in. And then it broke down . . . and I need a ambulance and a tow truck and a police car. . . . It was a bad guy that ran into me.* In response to this convincing account, the mechanic agreed to send two tow trucks. Another function of such embedded narratives is to justify a contested action or an objection. When her partner protested it, a five-year-old girl defended her appropriation of the car by saying *I'm supposed to drive it over your house. I am, because I drived it somewhere and I came back.* This concern with justifying present activities on the basis of prior events and thus providing "reasonable" motivations for the characters is displayed not only in pretend play but also in the narratives produced by older children. It is only one of the features contributing to the increasing length and complexity of both conversational narratives and pretend play episodes during the later preschool and early elementary school years.

Comparison of narratives and the construction and enactment of pretend scenarios reveals a number of similar and probably related trends. In both, the plot thickens. Additional ordered events are linked and related in increasingly varied ways (not only by the ordering of events in time but also by the relations of condition or contingency, physical and psychological causality, and consequences or outcomes). More of the optional components of narrative structure (introduction, abstract of action, and setting) and more of the possible components of pretend scenarios (the use of confederates to avert a threat) are added to story and to play performances. The variety of different types of narratives produced by the children Alison Preece observed is paralleled by the versatility with which older preschoolers can depict either everyday, fantastic, or even nonsensical events, assuming familiar, character, or occupational roles. Also, just as children learn to slip narratives into ongoing conversations, they learn to add narratives having different functions to the flow of pretend play. Narratives and pretend episodes alike become more clearly differentiated from their conversational and interactional contexts. Both become more explicitly framed as entities distinct from other ways of talking and interacting that children may command, and both become less subject to interruptions or distractions from the immediate environment. Both, in effect, reveal the child's increasing ability to produce autonomous, or decontextualized, texts—texts that can stand on their own and be interpreted without reference to information from the immediate physical environment. This last developmental trend depends, of course, on the child's cognitive ability to infer what a partner may know about a topic or about "what may be expected to happen," so that the speaker can provide just enough information to communicate effectively.

Children's facility in producing and understanding narrative plays an important role in how successfully they participate in school-based literacy tasks. Narratives, especially those that children encounter in school or are expected to produce in school-related contexts, exhibit certain uses of language that contribute to the formation of autonomous texts. Even in "show and tell" exercises, children are encouraged to use pronouns whose referents are introduced within the text and to provide the background information listeners need. In addition, teachers' comments model other features of language appropriate to the task (for example, clauses linked by conjunctions) and their prompting questions can often elicit important structural components, such as the details of the setting (*Where/when did you get the . . .*) or the outcome (*And what do you do with it?*). Since narrative time extends beyond the present moment of speaking, reaching back into the past and sometimes forward into the future, understanding and producing literate texts demands a variety of linguistic techniques for handling the temporal ordering of events. Although learning to read and write involves many types of knowledge and skill, a major prerequisite is previous familiarity and experience with the linguistic characteristics of autonomous texts. Several investigators are now attempting to discover whether the language children use in more mature social pretend play resembles the decontextualized language that characterizes narrative and other genres of literate language.

One such study carried out by Anthony Pellegrini examined the use of some of the characteristics of literate language in the speech of four- and five-year-old children engaged in dyadic play.[17] In complex sociodramatic pretend play (play in which several fantasy schemes were integrated into complex episodes), children tended to use more literate features in their conversation than when they were occupied in construction play or in other types of social interaction. Specifically, they more often used pronouns referring to elements that had already been explicitly introduced within the text and did so most often when they made ideational transformations. They also used more causal and temporal conjunctions, especially when they transformed real situations into fantasy ones. In addition, children used a greater number of elaborated noun phrases and future tense verbs during pretend play as well as more past tense verbs, which occurred primarily in exchanges in which the children were dealing with a misunderstanding or disagreement about the pretend situation. It may well be the case that children who are more familiar with narrative models are also more attracted to complex pretend play and better able to engage in the construction of extended fantastic or sociodramatic episodes. It is also likely that the very activity of pretending, with its unique cognitive and interactive demands, elicits language from the participants that shares a number of features with the language that characterizes autonomous texts.

Early experiences with books—with bedtime stories or reading aloud with a caregiver—are an important influence on children's subsequent ability to produce and understand texts and on some of the skills that will later contribute to their success in school-based tasks. For example, learning to provide verbal definitions is vital to classroom work, but it is a skill that develops relatively late in the elementary school period. One two-year-old whom we observed at home for several months had a very good start on the appropriate forms and uses of this complex skill. She and her mother were reading *Cinderella*, obviously not for the first time since the child had memorized some of the lines and correctly completed several sentences her mother left unfinished. When her mother read the part in which Cinderella is forbidden to go to the ball and they both looked at the picture of Cinderella alone in front of the fireplace, the child commented rather softly to herself, *Weeping is crying*, remembering the definition of weeping that her mother had given her during a previous reading when she had asked *What's weeping?*

Even learning nursery rhymes has recently been found to be related to the development of phonological skills and to subsequent success in learning to read. P. E. Bryant and his associates conducted a longitudinal study of children over a three-year period, beginning when they were 3:4.[18] The researchers reasoned that familiarity with rhyme, in which only one sound unit varies (for example, *Hickory dickory*), and alliteration, in which initial sounds are repeated (for example, *Baa-baa black sheep*), should increase children's sensitivity to sound units, which in turn should facilitate the task of relating written and spoken forms. (Rhyme and alliteration, of course, are among the construction principles children use in their own spontaneous play with the phonological system of language; for examples, see pages 68–70). They found that children's knowledge of nursery rhymes at three years of age predicted their success in reading and spelling two to three years later, as they entered elementary school. Familiarity with nursery rhymes appears to have facilitated the children's detection of the sound patterns of rhyme, which led them to recognize phonological units, a skill that helped them learn to read.

Activities conducted just for fun, telling stories, reciting nursery rhymes, reading books, playing with language, and constructing episodes of pretend play can have important repercussions for more serious achievements, such as acquiring literacy skills. All these experiences provide opportunities to recognize and to manipulate the linguistic components, textual properties, and communicative possibilities of language, skills that will play a role in the acquisition of reading and writing skills.

As this book has attempted to show, play takes diverse forms that change and become elaborated as the child matures. The facts lead to the consensus that it is difficult, if not impossible, to propose any single or uniform function for play in the life of a child or an immature animal. Playing with different resources at different levels of development will obviously have varied functions. Susanna Millar has suggested that the usefulness of play activities is related to their tendency to occur at relatively early stages in the organization of each of the child's systems of behavior.[19] Because playing is voluntarily controlled activity (executed in a way in which imperfect achievement is minimally dangerous), its effects are probably intricately related to the child's mastery and integration of her experiences.

Although playful activities generally derive from nonplay behavior patterns, those patterns need not be mature or complete to serve as a basis for play. They must, however, be sufficiently well controlled to be repeated, varied, and performed in such a way that their intent is signaled: the nonliteral orientation must be communicated. To say that play rests on the nonplay repertoire of behavior does not imply that the influence is necessarily unidirectional. A behavior pattern performed in the simulative mode can be elaborated and combined with other similarly "displaced" patterns. When the behavior is next performed in a nonplay mode, it may be more skilled, better integrated, and associated with a richer or wider range of meaning. In this way play can contribute to the expertise of the player and to his effectiveness in the nonplay world, whether that be in the area of his social relationships with other children or in the competencies that facilitate the development of literacy.

Finally, play has considerable value for students of child development. Some uses are obvious. For example, the changing forms of play, which tend to reflect newly acquired abilities, are associated with the course of normal growth and maturation. The failure of play to evolve—to become more complex and differentiated—often signals the existence of developmental problems. Less obvious, however, is that the study of spontaneous play can provide a rich source of information about the nature of a child's competence. Children at play enact or represent knowledge of their social and material world they cannot verbalize explicitly or demonstrate in the setting of experimental tasks. As long as *we* do not interpret their behavior overliterally, we can learn much about children's concepts of social rules and obligations, their understanding of the physical environment, and their knowledge of language structure—about all of the critically human resources at their command.

References

1 What Is Play?

1. Peter Reynolds, "Play, Language and Human Evolution," in Jerome Bruner, Allison Jolly, and Kathy Sylva, eds., *Play: Its Role in Development and Evolution* (Harmondsworth: Penguin, 1976).
2. Jerome Bruner, "The Nature and Uses of Immaturity," *American Psychologist*, 1972, *27*, 687–708.
3. Catherine Garvey, "Some Properties of Social Play," *Merrill-Palmer Quarterly*, 1974, *20*, 163–180.
4. Jean Piaget, *Play, Dreams and Imitation in Childhood* (London: Routledge, 1951; New York: Norton, 1962).

2 The Natural History of the Smile

1. Alan Sroufe and J. P. Wunsch, "The Development of Laughter in the First Year of Life," *Child Development*, 1972, *43*, 1326–1344.
2. Florence Justin, "A Genetic Study of Laughter Provoking Stimuli," *Child Development*, 1932, *3*, 114–135.
3. Lawrence Sherman, "An Ecological Study of Glee in Small Groups of Preschool Children," *Child Development*, 1975, *46*, 53–61.

3 Play with Motion and Interaction

1. Piaget, *Play, Dreams and Imitation in Childhood*, p. 91.
2. Daniel Stern, "Mother and Infant at Play: The Dyadic Interaction Involving Facial, Vocal and Gaze Behaviors," in Michael Lewis and Leonard Rosenblum, eds., *The Effect of the Infant on Its Caregiver* (New York: Wiley, 1974).
3. Irenaus Eibl-Eibesfeldt, "Concepts of Ethology and Their Significance in the Study of Human Behavior," in Harold

Stevenson, Eckhard Hess, and Harriet Rheingold, eds., *Early Behavior* (New York: Wiley, 1967).

4. Harry Harlow, "Agemate and Peer Affectional Systems," in D. S. Lehrman, Robert Hinde, and E. Shaw, eds., *Advances in the Study of Behavior*, vol. 2 (London and New York: Academic Press, 1970).

5. Meredith West, "Social Play in the Domestic Cat," *American Zoologist*, 1974, *14*, 127–136.

6. Marc Bekoff, "Social Play in Coyotes, Wolves and Dogs," *Bio Sciences*, 1974, *24*, 225–230.

7. Carol Eckerman, Judith Whatley, and Stuart Kutz, "The Growth of Social Play with Peers During the Second Year of Life," *Developmental Psychology*, 1975, *11*, 42–49.

8. Edward Mueller and Deborah Vandell, "Infant-infant Interaction," in Joy Osofsky, ed., *Handbook of Infant Development* (New York: Wiley, 1979).

9. Wanda Bronson, "Developments in Behavior with Agemates During the Second Year of Life," in Michael Lewis and Leonard Rosenblum, eds., *Friendship and Peer Relations* (New York: Wiley, 1975).

10. Nicholas Blurton-Jones, "Categories of Child-Child Interaction," in Nicholas Blurton-Jones, ed., *Ethological Studies of Child Behavior* (Cambridge: Cambridge University Press, 1972). Peter Smith and Kevin Connolly, "Patterns of Play and Social Interaction in Preschool Children," in Blurton-Jones, ed., *Ethological Studies of Child Behavior*.

11. William Nydegger and Corinne Nydegger, "Tarong, an Ilocos Barrio in the Philippines," in Beatrice and John Whiting, eds., *Six Cultures: Studies of Child Rearing* (New York: Wiley, 1963).

4 Play with Objects

1. Jerome Bruner, "The Growth of Representational Processes in Childhood," in Jeremy Anglin, ed., *Beyond the Information Given* (London: Allen & Unwin, 1974; New York: Norton, 1974).

2. Marianne Lowe, "Trends in the Development of Representational Play in Infants from One to Three Years: An Observational Study," *Journal of Child Psychology*, 1975, *16*, 33–48.

3. Greta Fein, "A Transformational Analysis of Pretending," *Developmental Psychology*, 1975, *11*, 291–296.

4. Corinne Hutt, "Exploration and Play in Children," *Symposia of the Zoological Society of London*, 1966, *18*, 61–81.

5. Kathy Sylva, "Play and Learning," in Barbara Tizard and David Harvey, eds., *The Biology of Play* (London: Heinemann, 1976; Philadelphia: Lippincott, 1976).

6. Edward Mueller and Thomas Lucas, "A Developmental Analysis of Peer Interaction among Toddlers," in Lewis and Rosenblum, eds., *Friendship and Peer Relations*.

7. M. Waterhouse and H. Waterhouse, "Primate Ethology and Human Social Behavior," in Richard Michael and John Crook, eds., *Comparative Ecology and Behavior of Primates* (New York: Academic Press, 1973).

8. Eckerman et al., "The Growth of Social Play with Peers during the Second Year of Life."

9. Harriet Rheingold and Kaye Cook, "The Contents of Boys' and Girls' Rooms as an Index of Parents' Behavior," *Child Development*, 1975, *46*, 459–463.

10. Margaret Parten, "Social Play among Preschool Children," *Journal of Abnormal and Social Psychology*, 1933, *28*, 136–147.

11. Erik Erikson, "Sex Differences in Play Configurations of Pre-Adolescents," *American Journal of Ortho-Psychiatry*, 1951, *21*, 667–692.

12. Jules and Zunia Henry, *"The Doll Play of Pilaga Indian Children* (New York: Vintage Books, 1974).

5 *Play with Language*

1. Kornei Chukovsky, *From Two to Five* (Berkeley: University of California Press, 1963).

2. Iona and Peter Opie, *The Lore and Language of Schoolchil-*

dren (Oxford and New York: Oxford University Press, 1959).

3. Harriet Johnson, *Children in the Nursery School* (New York: Agathon Press, 1972).

4. Elinor Keenan, "Conversational Competence in Children," *Journal of Child Language*, 1974, *1*, 163–183.

5. Ruth Weir, *Language in the Crib* (The Hague: Mouton, 1972).

6. Chukovsky, *From Two to Five*, p. 96.

7. Anne Davison, "Linguistic Play and Language Acquisition," in *Papers and Reports on Child Language Development* (special issue; Sixth Child Language Research Forum, Stanford, 1974).

8. John Austin, *How to Do Things with Words* (Cambridge: Harvard University Press, 1962).

6 Play with Social Materials

1. Eric Klinger, "The Development of Imaginative Behavior: Implications of Play for a Theory of Fantasy," *Psychological Bulletin*, 1967, *72*, 277–298.

2. Michael Halliday, *Explorations in the Functions of Language* (London: Arnold, 1973).

3. Gustav Ichheiser, *Appearances and Realities* (San Francisco: Jossey-Bass, 1970).

4. Harvey Sacks, "On the Analyzability of Stories by Children," in John Gumperz and Dell Hymes, eds., *Directions in Sociolinguistics* (New York: Holt, Rinehart and Winston, 1972).

5. Lev Vygotsky, "Play and Its Role in the Mental Development of the Child," *Soviet Psychology*, 1967, *5*, 6–18.

6. Jerome Singer, ed., *The Child's World of Make-Believe* (New York: Academic Press, 1973).

7. Robin Herron and Brian Sutton-Smith, eds., *Child's Play* (New York: Wiley, 1971).

8. Sarah Smilanksy, *The Effects of Sociodramatic Play on Disadvantaged Preschool Children* (New York: Wiley, 1968).

Dina Feitelson, "Cross-Cultural Studies," in Tizard and Harvey, *The Biology of Play*.

9. Rivka Eifermann, "Social Play in Childhood," in Herron and Sutton-Smith, eds., *Child's Play*.

10. Joan Freyberg, "Increasing the Imaginative Play of Urban Disadvantaged Children through Systematic Training," in Singer, ed., *The Child's World of Make-Believe*.

7 Play with Rules

1. Iona and Peter Opie, *Children's Games in Street and Playground* (Oxford and New York: Oxford University Press, 1969).

2. Jerome Bruner and V. Sherwood, "Peekaboo and the Learning of Rule Structures," in Jerome Bruner, Allison Jolly, and Kathy Sylva, eds., *Play: Its Role in Development and Evolution* (Harmondsworth: Penguin, 1976).

3. Roger Caillois, *Man, Play and Games* (New York: Free Press, 1961).

4. Erving Goffman, *Interaction Ritual* (New York: Doubleday Anchor, 1967; Harmondsworth: Penguin, 1971).

5. William Labov, *Studies in the Black English Vernacular* (Philadelphia: University of Pennsylvania Press, 1972).

9 Learning to Play

1. Tom Power and Ross Parke, "Play as a Context for Early Learning: Lab and Home Analyses," in Luis Laosa and Irving Sigel, eds., *Families as Learning Environments for Children* (New York: Plenum, 1982).

2. Arietta Slade, "A Longitudinal Study of Maternal Involvement and Symbolic Play during the Toddler Period," *Child Development*, 1987, *58*, 367–375.

3. Robert Kavanaugh, Sue Whittington, and Mark Cerbone, "Mothers' Use of Fantasy in Speech to Young Children," *Journal of Child Language*, 1983, *10*, 45–56.

4. Wendy Haight and Peggy Miller, *The Ecology and Devel-*

opment of Pretend Play, Play in Society Series (New York: SUNY Press, forthcoming).

5. Peggy Miller and Catherine Garvey, "Mother-Baby Role Play: Its Origins in Social Support," in Inge Bretherton, ed., *Symbolic Play: The Development of Social Understanding* (New York: Academic Press, 1984).

6. Judy Dunn and Naomi Dale, "I a Daddy: 2-Year-Olds' Collaboration in Joint Pretend with Sibling and with Mother," in Inge Bretherton, ed., *Symbolic Play: The Development of Social Understanding* (New York: Academic Press, 1984).

7. Patricia Zukow, "Siblings as Effective Socializing Agents: Evidence from Central Mexico," in Patricia Zukow, ed., *Sibling Interaction across Cultures* (New York: Springer-Verlag, 1989); Suzanne Gaskins, "Symbolic Play in a Mayan Village" (Paper presented to the Annual Meeting of the Association for the Study of Play, 1989).

8. Joann Farver, "Cultural Differences in American and Mexican Mother-Child Play" (Paper presented to the Biennial Meeting of the Society for Research in Child Development, Kansas City, 1989).

9. Holly Giffin, "The Coordination of Meaning in the Creation of a Shared Make-Believe Reality," in Inge Bretherton, ed., *Symbolic Play: The Development of Social Understanding* (New York: Academic Press, 1984).

10. Catherine Garvey and Thayer Kramer, "The Language of Social Pretending," *Developmental Review,* 1989, *9*, 364–382.

11. Greta Fein, "Mind, Meaning and Affect: Proposals for a Theory of Pretense," *Developmental Review*, 1989, *9*, 345–363.

12. Lisabeth Fisher DiLalla and Malcolm Watson, "Differentiation of Fantasy and Reality: Preschoolers' Reactions to Interruptions in Their Play," *Developmental Psychology*, 1988, *24*, 286–291.

10 Play and the Real World

1. Thomas Kochman, "The Boundary between Play and Nonplay in Black Verbal Dueling," *Language in Society*, 1983, *12*, 239–337.
2. Shirley Brice Heath, *Ways with Words: Language, Life, and Work in Communities and Classrooms* (Cambridge: Cambridge University Press, 1983).
3. Shlomo Ariel and Irene Sever, "Children's Play: From Bedouins to Boy Scouts," in Helen Schwartzman, ed., *Play and Culture* (West Point, N.Y.: Leisure Press, 1980).
4. Dennie Wolf and S. H. Grollman, "Ways of Playing: Individual Differences in Imaginative Style," in Kenneth Rubin and Deborah Pepler, eds., *The Play of Children: Current Theory and Research* (Basel: S. Karger, 1982).
5. Alan Leslie, "Some Implication of Pretense for Mechanisms Underlying the Child's Theory of Mind," in Janet Astington, Paul Harris, and David Olson, eds., *Developing Theories of Mind* (New York: Cambridge University Press, 1988).
6. Barrie Thorne, "Boys and Girls Together . . . but Mostly Apart: Gender Arrangements in Elementary Schools," in William Hartup and Zick Rubin, eds., *Relationships and Development* (Hillsdale, N.J.: Erlbaum, 1989).
7. Betty Black, "Interactive Pretense: Social and Symbolic Skills in Preschool Play Groups," *Merrill Palmer Quarterly*, 1989, *35*, 379–397.
8. Jennifer Connolly, Anna Beth Doyle, and Flavia Cheschin, "Forms and Functions of Social Fantasy Play in Preschoolers," in M. Liss, ed., *Children's Play: Sex Differences and Acquisition of Cognitive and Social Skills* (New York: Academic Press, 1983).
9. Anna Beth Doyle, Jennifer Connolly, and Louis-Paul Rivest, "The Effect of Playmate Familiarity on the Social Interactions of Young Children," *Child Development*, 1980, *51*, 217–223.
10. Catherine Emihovich, "The Intimacy of Address: Friend-

ship Markers in Children's Social Play," *Language in Society*, 1981, *10*, 189–199.

11. Jeffrey Parker and John Gottman, "Social and Emotional Development in a Relational Context: Friendship Interaction from Early Childhood to Adolescence," in Thomas Berndt and Gary Ladd, eds., *Peer Relationships in Child Development* (New York: Wiley, 1989).

12. Nancy Hazen and Betty Black, "Preschool Peer Communication Skills: The Role of Social Status and Interaction Context," *Child Development*, 1989, *60*, 867–876; and Martha Putallaz, "Predicting Children's Sociometric Status from their Behavior," *Child Development*, 1983, *54*, 1417–29.

13. Katherine Nelson, ed., *Narratives from the Crib* (Cambridge: Harvard University Press, 1989).

14. Robert Scholes, "Language, Narrative, and Anti-Narrative," in W. J. Mitchell, ed., *On Narrative* (Chicago: University of Chicago Press, 1981).

15. Alison Preece, "The Range of Narrative Forms Conversationally Produced by Young Children," *Journal of Child Language*, 1987, *14*, 353–373.

16. Jean Umiker-Sebeok, "Preschool Children's Intraconversational Narratives," *Journal of Child Language*, 1979, *6*, 91–110.

17. Anthony Pellegrini, "Relations between Preschool Children's Symbolic Play and Literate Behavior," in Lee Galda and Anthony Pellegrini, eds., *Play, Language, and Stories: The Development of Children's Literate Behavior* (Norwood, N.J.: Ablex, 1985).

18. P. E. Bryant, L. Bradley, M. Maclean, and J. Crossland, "Nursery Rhymes, Phonological Skills, and Reading," *Journal of Child Language*, 1989, *16*, 407–428.

19. Susanna Millar, *The Psychology of Play*, (Harmondsworth: Penguin, 1968).

Suggested Reading

Inge Bretherton, ed., *Symbolic Play: The Development of Social Understanding* (New York: Academic Press, 1984). A collection of original papers by prominent investigators that report on their new research on toddler and preschool play. The papers are grouped by two major topics: cooperative symbolic play and symbolic play with toys and words; virtually all of them stress social context as an important influence on play. The editor provides a thoughtful introduction that discusses the uses and significance of symbolic play.

Jerome Bruner, Allison Jolly, and Kathy Sylva, eds., *Play: Its Role in Development and Evolution* (Harmondsworth: Penguin, 1976). A collection of writings on play from many different sources—scientists, philosophers, artists—organized under four major topics: the evolutionary context; play and the world of objects and tools; play and the social world; play and the world of symbols. This eclectic and imaginative compilation provides an excellent picture of the diversity and pervasiveness of play in nature and in civilization.

Vivian Gussin Paley, *Mollie Is Three: Growing Up in School* (Chicago and London: University of Chicago Press, 1986); and, by the same author, *Bad Guys Don't Have Birthdays: Fantasy Play at Four* (Chicago and London: University of Chicago Press, 1988). These two slim volumes by a sensitive and astute teacher provide an intimate picture of the forms and functions of play in the nursery school. Vivian Paley records the spontaneous conversations and play of children, focusing in each book on one child. She traces the growth of each child over the period of a year, showing, in detailed and delightful transcriptions of the talk, just how intricately play and social and emotional development are intertwined.

Jean Piaget, *Play, Dreams and Imitation in Childhood* (London: Routledge, 1951; New York: Norton, 1962). One of the best "personalized" introductions to Piaget's unique and influential ideas about the progression from infancy to childhood to adolescence. Although his discussions on the dynamics of development make rather difficult reading, Piaget's text is filled with detailed and fascinating observations of the day-to-day behavior of his own three children, accounts that can assist parents in understanding and enjoying their own child's progress.

Kenneth Rubin, Greta Fein, and Brian Vandenberg, "Play," in E. M. Hetherington, ed., *Carmichael's Manual of Child Psychology: Social Development*, 4th ed. (New York: Wiley, 1983). A critical and comprehensive review of the psychological literature on play, in fact, the first treatment of this topic to appear in the four editions of this important manual. It covers a number of topics not discussed in this book or in the other suggested readings, including media and curriculum influences on play, play in handicapped children, and the effects of training studies.

Peter K. Smith, ed., *Play in Animals and Humans* (New York and Oxford: Basil Blackwell, 1984). A collection of papers by British, Canadian, and American investigators. It contains interesting summaries of ethological research on ungulates, cats, rodents, and monkeys, chapters on object play, problem-solving, and creativity in children and on rough-and-tumble play, and a valuable paper on the little-researched topic of imaginary playmates. Several papers deal with play and games beyond the period of childhood. The editor's commentaries on each section highlight the problems and promises of cross-disciplinary research on play and its functions.

Credits

Index